Critical Acclaim for *Take Charge* and *Find a Job You Reall*

"Whatever you do or have done, this is a great book to help _____ ~~take~~ a look at yourself in the context of the world around you – and what you should do in it. At any time, people need help to realise their ambitions and skills, but never has this been more so than now. Corina Grace has put together in a single place much that is needed to support people at this time." – *Mohan Yogendran, Partner, Rockpools, a UK market leader in executive recruitment, interim management and professional development*

"Dr Grace has presented us with an engaging toolkit with her latest publication. Readers are effortlessly taken through a series of exercises which help calibrate your strengths, creating a roadmap allowing you to take control and plan your career. This very readable volume is a worthy investment in your career, and you can be confident it will yield long-term benefits." – *Joe Ryan, Director, EMEA Human Resources, Johnson & Johnson*

"Dr. Corina Grace has woven her career experiences and those of her clients into a practical guide. Timely, well constructed and extremely engaging, this workbook could change your life." – *Dr Paul Mooney, President, National College of Ireland*

"This book is an essential guide for anyone not yet on the career ladder, anyone beginning their career, changing their career or even thinking about doing something different. This book will really help individuals to gain a greater degree of personal insight and understand how they can market themselves and create that mindset for success!" – *Denise Banks, Head of Learning & Development, Accenture*

"This is a must read book for anyone who is serious about getting ahead in their life and their career. Packed with advice and complete with exercises and examples, *Take Charge of Your Career* is written for people both looking for work and for those already in a job – Brilliant." – *Dr. Alexandra Groess, Head of HR Allianz Re, Allianz Global Corporate & Specialty AG – Munich*

"Dr Grace has the rare ability to combine depth and practicality. This book stimulates genuine self-insight at the same time as it gives you the practcal wherewhithal to get on with the job of sorting out your job." – *Chris Blakeley, Director, Waverley Learning (UK)*

"If you really want to know why you are where you are at in your life or your career at the moment, read this. It will enlighten you as to how you got there … and help you figure out how to get to wherever you want to go next." – *Alan Kelly, Managing Director, Data Ireland Limited*

"In her role as a senior associate consultant with OPP, one of Europe's leading firms of business psychologists, Corina Grace has provided invaluable input on major senior level assignments. Corina brings many strengths, foremost being her ability to generate innovative, meaningful yet practical solutions based on her own extensive professional experience combined with her comprehensive knowledge of relevant academic research in the subject area. Knowing that this same combination prevails in her new book makes it a 'must read' for anyone who is considering a career move, or for those of us who are involved in advising others on career planning and development issues." – Dom Crotty M.Sc. (Mgmt), County Manager, OPP Ireland

"Forget the theory ... this is a sound practical workbook that will help anybody to take charge of and manage their career. Indispensable in these turbulent times, whether you are starting out, wanting to develop your career or are trying to get your career 'back on track'." – John O'Hehir, Strategic HR Director

"Corina brings a truly holistic and energetic approach to any project. I think it is wonderful that she has taken the time to share her wealth of experience, knowledge and insight in this way. We will all benefit from this very 'grounded workbook', from the individual seeking a 'best-fit job' to those of us involved in employee development and career planning." – Kate Costelloe, Head of Learning & Development, Beaumont Hospital

"Taking charge of your career plan is the single most important action you can take on the path to a successful and rewarding career. Corina has presented us with a well structured, challenging and enjoyable way to discover our ideal career route. The approach is built on the principle of the job fitting me rather than me fitting the job. This is a must read for job seekers, job changers or any one who is taking time out to chart their careers plans." – Denis Kelly, Manager, HR Development Group, ESB Power Generation

"Corina has a great insight into people and how they can work to their full potential in a work environment. Her process of deciding what one is most suited to is simply brilliant. Everyone should begin by finding out what they are good at and what they like doing as it is the key to long-term success. Corina's book gets you to think about all these vitally important factors before you make a decision. It is not surprising that this formula leads to success as it is the secret of all success." – Rachel Naughton, Head of Corporate Business Development and Strategy, Corporate Banking Ireland, AIB

"Warning: Reading this book could seriously enhance your career prospects!" – Mark Graham, Head of Employee Relations, An Post

TAKE CHARGE OF YOUR CAREER
... AND FIND A JOB YOU REALLY LOVE!

The Essential Handbook for
Job-Seekers and Job-Changers

Dr Corina Grace

The Liffey Press

Published by
The Liffey Press
Ashbrook House
10 Main Street, Raheny,
Dublin 5, Ireland
www.theliffeypress.com

© 2009 Dr Corina Grace

A catalogue record of this book is
available from the British Library.

ISBN 978-1-905785-33-9

Printed in Ireland by Colour Books.

Contents

ABOUT THE AUTHOR

Dr. Corina Grace is one of Europe's foremost career development experts, with almost two decades' experience of helping multinational organisations build their business capability through developing and releasing the potential of their people. Corina, who is Managing Director of Grace Consulting, has worked with a who's who of major multinational clients advising them on talent management, releasing leadership potential and thriving during times of change. A psychology graduate from UCD and Queens University, Belfast, Corina has that rare talent of being able to combine her in-depth knowledge and expertise in psychology with her experience as a Senior HR Change Management Consultant. As Practice Director with Waverley Learning, a UK consultancy firm specialising in Leadership Development, she co-presents their very successful Crossroads & Executive Retreats. In this book Corina shares with you a host of key learnings which will help you find your vocation rather than your job, letting you share your true gifts with the world. In today's new economy, where we are faced with the need to reassess the very concepts of job and career, Corina's advice and guidance will prove invaluable in helping you decide how you wish to spend your working life.

For my husband Brian, for his encouragement, love and support and without whom this book would never have been written – "Always".

Part One

Introduction and Overview

1

Introduction

"We must all obey the great law of change. It is the most powerful law of nature."
– Edmund Burke

DEALING WITH THE CHANGING JOB MARKET

In the last couple of years we have seen the very core and fabric of our working and personal lives change. The nature of our careers is qualitatively shifting and we need to be ready to respond. Unfortunately, in today's job market the news is all doom and gloom with downsizing, outsourcing, mergers and job losses becoming everyday occurrences. This spells the end of the world of work as we know it. The days of the permanent, pensionable job are all but at an end. Few people entering the workforce in the last 10 years will end their career with the same employer they started out with. In fact, it is believed that most people will have changed jobs at least 10 times before they retire.

Many authors have been talking about the changing world of work for some time now. One such author, William Bridges, in his book *Job Shift*, argues that the nature of work is shifting and "the job" as we know it is fast disappearing, requiring us to take a radically different perspective on how to make a living. Bridges highlights a number of factors which spells the demise of "the job", factors that are prevalent today, including the fall in the number of permanent jobs due to the increase in contract work, outsourcing and technology. Matrix management structures and de-centralisation have also fundamentally shifted the way people work, requiring more flexibility and the development of more diverse skills. According to Bridges, there is still as much work to be done, it just doesn't fit nearly into the tidy box of "a job".

3

Tom Peters writes in a similar vain in his book titled *The Brand Called You*. He focuses on the decline of "the career" and believes that we need to radically rethink how we view our working lives. For Peters, careers should no longer be viewed as a means of moving up the corporate ladder, but instead should be viewed more like a "checkerboard, or even a maze", and like the moves in a checkerboard or maze your career can move sideways, forwards, diagonally or even backwards when required. He further adds that "a career is a portfolio of projects that teach you new skills, gain you new expertise, develop new capabilities, grow your colleague set, and constantly reinvent you as a brand".

If we are to succeed in this new reality, we now have to see ourselves as "Creating the Brand Called You", as Tom Peters so aptly describes it, or as Bridges says, as "Creating You and Co.". Basically you are now the CEO of your own career and that is why you need to think and act like a CEO of the brand called YOU. Some of the actions you need to begin to take relate to:

- Having a powerful vision for you, your career and your life
- Developing a competitive product portfolio – YOU
- Designing a strategy and an action plan
- Branding, marketing and selling your product portfolio – YOU
- Creating a demand for your product portfolio –YOU.

It may seem daunting at first but the good news is that this workbook has all the tools necessary to get you started. With a little forethought and preparation, and admittedly some hard work, you can begin to map out the best possible plan for your career, and find the job that you really love. This workbook brings together some of the best tools in career planning and job-seeking available. It gives you a comprehensive and practical career design and goal-setting framework, and includes tools that some of the best business managers and executives use to achieve their own goals. This workbook will give you everything that you need to set out on your own journey to success and fulfilment in your career.

More specifically, this workbook will:

- Provide you with a comprehensive picture of YOU, your brand and your product portfolio by learning about your own personal style and work preferences, your unique selling points, your values, life choices and specific gifts and talents.
- Having pulled together a comprehensive picture of YOU, to then begin to think creatively as to where YOU might fit in relation to the roles or jobs you might aspire to, or even more pertinent, how you might begin to shape and create your own perfect 'job' which matches your particular set of gifts, talents and interests.

- Give you an up-to-the minute development tool kit to assess and develop your capabilities against the qualities and skills that matter if you are to be successful irrespective of your chosen job or career path.

- Set YOU within a wider context and allow you to dream on a broader canvas about the vision you have for you, your life and your career. And begin the process of energising you to manifest that vision in real and tangible ways by providing the tools and techniques to successfully market and sell yourself and ultimately secure the job of your dreams.

- Most importantly, it will give you the tools and techniques that all top professionals and athletes use to cultivate the mindset for success, and which you can apply in your own life to get the results you so richly deserve.

CREATING SUCCESS IN YOUR CAREER, DEVELOPMENT AND JOB

So where do you start. Well Figure 1 outlines the three key sections covered in this workbook, which contains a range of activities that will give you a clear picture of all aspects important to your career, development and job search. These are outlined in greater detail below. Everything that you need in order to achieve in each of these areas is contained in this workbook.

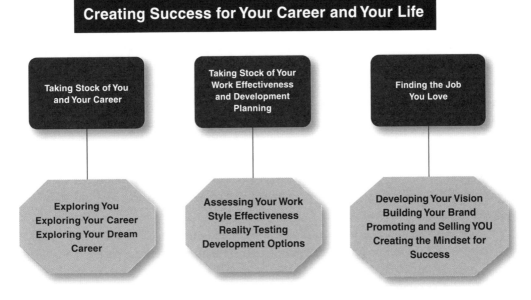

Figure 1: Outline of Three Key Sections Covered in This Book

Taking Stock of You and Your Career

In order to understand where you want to go it is important to take stock of where you have been, what you have to offer and how you would like to balance your life against your values and choices. Your pen picture should be as comprehensive as possible and reflect all strands in the fabric of your life, not just your career. The decisions you make about your career can have an impact on other dimensions of your life – just as the decisions you make in your personal life can affect your career. As a consequence, this section explores three important aspects: You, Your Career and Your Dream Career. Each of these sections asks you to accurately analyse and diagnose aspects of these areas. More specifically, it asks you explore your life and your values, how you can make the most of your current role whilst keeping an eye on your future career, and how to set inspiring goals which will keep you motivated and engaged.

The exercises in this section of the workbook will help you develop a greater awareness of what you need to do to keep all the dimensions of your life in healthy balance. But most importantly, it will begin to tease out your Brand and Product portfolio and help you identify your unique selling points or USPs.

Taking Stock of Your Work Effectiveness and Development Needs

Having an understanding of your style and preferences, and the skills you have acquired over time, is important, but equally important is knowing what makes for superior performance and how well you stack up against such criteria. This section contains a generic model called the Work Style Effectiveness Model (WSEM), which pulls together the key qualities and skills that matter in a career and which differentiates between average and superior performance. You will have the opportunity to assess yourself against this model and identify your talents and your development areas. Knowing your strengths and development needs will enable you to become more effective in your current role, and also provides you with core information necessary to sell yourself for any future roles you aspire to. This section also contains a comprehensive guide to soliciting feedback as well as a development section packed with ideas and suggestions on how you can develop in some of the sixteen areas contained in the WSEM.

The exercises in this section of the workbook will help you identify your key strengths and development needs against criteria that matters in a career. They will also provide you with a rich source of information as to how you can be truly successful and excel in any career you might aspire to.

Finding the Job that You Love

Credible CEOs knows the importance of developing a clear vision and strategy in order to be successful in a competitive environment, and the same holds true for getting the career and job of your dreams. So often we leave the future to chance, never fully clarifying what it is we want to achieve or what blueprint we want to follow. This section gives you the opportunity to create your vision for your life and to dream on a bigger canvas. You will be able to incorporate all that you have learnt in the previous two sections and map them into this vision, while at the same time building this vision into something which is deeper and more profound, and which is at the very core of who you are. This vision will guide and sustain you during the more challenging periods and will provide you with the momentum and the energy to keep reaching for the stars! Having identified your product portfolio – YOU – and mapped out your vision and the goals for achieving that vision, our attention turns to that all important topic of building your brand and marketing and selling yourself. There are a number of ground breaking exercises in this section which will help you market and sell yourself effectively and ultimately secure the job of your dreams. The guidelines and information provided will ensure not only that you stay the course, but that you achieve success.

The exercises in this section of the workbook will give you the competitive edge necessary to succeed in securing that job. It will provide you with exceptional tools to secure the job of your dreams and to manifest all that you desire.

Conclusion

Not all sections in this workbook will be equally relevant to you. Your personal career and life situation, age, position, values and the amount of time you have spent in your present position will determine the importance of particular questions you are asked about your career and the areas you need to explore in greater depth. The Guide to the Exercises in this section provides information about each of the exercises in this workbook and can help you identify the exercises which will be most helpful to you.

2

Using This Workbook

. . . .

"When old words die out on the tongue, new melodies break forth from the heart; and where the old tracks are lost, new country is revealed with its wonders."
– Rabindranath Tagore

. . . .

BRAINSTORM

Many people have problems in making career and development plans because they inhibit expressing their ideas and goals, telling themselves things like, "I could never achieve this", "that opportunity is not available to me", "this isn't feasible", and so on.

In working through these exercises, it is important to suspend judgement and to let your imagination flow. Use creative thinking, let your thoughts wander and dream about what your ideal job, life or work situation would be like. This is a fantasy exercise; don't think about obstacles and problems for now. First generate ideas without censoring your thoughts. Later you can sit back and evaluate how realistic they are.

PACE YOURSELF

Don't be deterred by the length of this workbook. Although it looks like considerable work it will not require many hours to complete. The best way to approach it is by completing one or two exercises at a time, set yourself a schedule over the next few weeks, and try to keep to it. You will probably get the best results if you can complete the entire workbook within a four to six week period. That way, you will still have your earlier findings clear in your mind as you complete the later exercises.

8

SPEND TIME/INVEST EFFORT

The benefits you will obtain from the materials in this workbook will be in direct proportion to the effort you put into completing them. Although it may be tempting to just read through the exercises and "complete them in your head", you will derive much greater benefit by sitting down, pencil in hand.

FOCUS ON AREAS MOST RELEVANT TO YOUR SITUATION

As already mentioned, not all sections of this workbook will be equally relevant to your own particular questions and concerns. Concentrate on those exercises which are most personally meaningful to you. The Guide to the Exercises which follows provides information about each of the exercises and what you will gain from completing it.

CONSULT OTHERS

Development and career planning requires integrating information about yourself – your interests, skills and potential – with information about any particular job or industry. You will have better information about yourself if you check your personal perceptions against those of people who know you well and have had an opportunity to observe you, for example, your friends, partner, colleagues and supervisor or manager.

Guide to the Exercises – 1

9

Exploring You

Understanding Your Personality Traits and Characteristics

It is important to get a pen picture of your personality and how you appear to others. According to personality theory, there is a strong relationship between your personality and your choice of career. This exercise will provide you with the opportunity to assess yourself against a set of personality traits, and identify what career best fits with your style and preference.

Clarifying Your Values

In completing this activity you will identify what is most important to you and what you want out of your life and career. You will develop criteria for determining personal and career goals and selecting the kind of position and working environment which best matches your needs and preferences. You will also evaluate the degree to which your present position meets your underlying values.

Lifestyle Satisfaction Assessment

Your career is only one important strand in the fabric of your life. This activity will help you evaluate how well you are balancing the different areas of your life along important dimensions related to life and career planning, and to develop lifestyle goals and plans to address identified areas for improvement.

Exploring Your Career

Identifying Sources of Satisfaction and Dissatisfaction in Your Job

This exercise will help you evaluate and clarify your feelings about the individual components of your job, and provide you with important information about your job preferences. As a result, you will be able to:

- Begin to develop specifications for modifying your present position to build in more of what you want and reduce aspects you find less satisfying.
- Develop guidelines and criteria for evaluating future career moves.

Career History Analysis

This activity will provide you with important information about:

- How your past positions have contributed to your development
- The skills and abilities you have acquired over your career
- Your underlying career orientations and preferences.

Note: For individuals who have held at least two positions.

EXPLORING YOUR DREAM CAREER

In looking at your career choices it is important to look to the future and to channel your dreams into your ideal job. In order to fully realise your potential you need to articulate what your long-terms goals and dreams are in this area. This exercise puts the results of your self-assessment together. In completing this exercise you will:

- Summarise key information about yourself which will help determine your ideal career direction

- Evaluate how well the features of your present position match with what you are ideally seeking and are suited for.

Guide to the Exercises – 2

ASSESSING YOUR WORK STYLE EFFECTIVENESS

This assessment will enable you to conduct a thorough analysis of your skills, knowledge and attitudes, and will help you to identify the skills you are strongest in and also those which need developing. This Work Style Effectiveness Model (WSEM) incorporates the key skills and qualities which differentiates superior performance in a role. Completing this questionnaire will help you answer such questions as:

- What are the distinctive characteristics of your work style?

- What elements of your work style are you strongest in?

- What elements of your work style do you need to develop in order to realise your full potential?

This is a flexible model and is not only relevant to your current role, but also to possible future roles.

REALITY TESTING: SOLICITING FEEDBACK FROM OTHERS

Career planning and development cannot be conducted in a vacuum. In order to set realistic goals you need feedback on how others perceive your strengths, skills, and general potential within the context of your current role or against your future aspirations. This activity tells you how to go about the process of testing the results of your self-assessment with people whose opinion you value who can give you an objective viewpoint.

DEVELOPMENT OPTIONS

This segment provides an outline on the tools available to help you develop your personal goals against the WSEM. The development options are drawn from a wide variety of sources which reflect best practice in the field of career management and development. There are hundreds of different actions that you can take to enhance and develop your talent and skills.

This segment also provides helpful guidelines and suggestions for evaluating your development options, setting meaningful and achievable development goals, and planning how to realise them.

Guide to the Exercises – 3

Finding the Job
You Love

Developing Your Vision

Building Your Brand

Promoting and Selling YOU

Creating the Mindset for Success

Developing Your Vision

Looking to the Future – What Do I Want?

This segment of the chapter asks the question, "what is it I really want for my life?" It is about pulling together all you have learned in this workbook as well as gaining greater perspective and insight into the dreams and visions you have for your life. Having completed this segment you will have a clear sense of where you are headed, which you can refer to time and again to ensure you are on the right track.

Programming for Success

The goal of this section is for you to optimise the use of your time and resources and to get every aspect of your mind working for your benefit. It will also help ensure that you are developing in the areas that are important. To do so, you will need to ensure that you are developing the areas that will:

*   Have a positive impact on all aspects of your life and career
*   Give you greater personal satisfaction in your career and finding a job you love.

This section provides you with the opportunity to assess your goals over the next one to three years and begins the process of identifying what will help you succeed and what might hold you back.

Building Your Brand

In this chapter you will learn how to build a personal brand and begin the process of marketing yourself. It outlines in three easy steps how you can build your own Personal Marketing Plan, from devising your personal brand to deciding on your market and using effective channels to getting you noticed.

Promoting and Selling YOU

This chapter has practical tools and techniques for writing that all important CV and selling yourself at interview. It will give you all the resources you will need to get you in the door of a prospective employer, and once in that door to make a great impression. There is a wealth of information on "do's and don'ts" when it comes to writing a CV and there are a number of templates you can use to create your own CV. It also provides you with insights on analysing job advertisements, thus enabling you to make the right decision on whether this is the job for you and to tailor your CV and your interview to match those role requirements. This chapter also has a comprehensive section on preparing for a job interview.

CREATING THE MINDSET FOR SUCCESS

It is critical that you don't allow doubts or fears to erode your confidence and ultimately your dreams. With so much negativity around you can easily find your motivation and energy dissipating. This chapter first looks at how you can future-proof your career, and then examines some of the factors which can impact on your motivation, providing you with five strategies to help you to stay on-track and reach your destination!

Part Two

Taking Stock of You and your Career

Exploring You
Exploring Your Career
Exploring Your Dream Career

3

Exploring You

INTRODUCTION

Assessment is a great way to explore your career opportunities. It provides you with information that can be invaluable in deciding what you want from your career. There are many different assessments you can take, like personality profiles, values profiles, and interests and skills profiles. Each provides you with a different perspective of who you are and what is important to you. Combined you get a fuller appreciation of all the different facets of your make-up and style. Assessment tools have other uses; they can help you evaluate your current career and help with any development gaps that you may have. This chapter on Exploring You contains three assessment tools which look at your personality style and preference, your personal and work values and how well you balance the different aspects of your life. It will provide a comprehensive picture of where your preferences lie in relation to your career, what is important to you both in your work and personal life, and it will help you chart out a balance between you life and your career.

More specifically, the tools will help you to:

- Assess your personality style and preferences and identify those roles which will bring out the best of who you are
- Explore your core values, both personally and in a work setting, and evaluate the degree to which your present position meets your underlying values

- Evaluate how well you are balancing the different areas of your life along important dimensions related to life and career planning, and develop lifestyle goals and plans to address identified areas for improvement.

PERSONALITY TRAITS AND CHARACTERISTICS

The daily musings that we have on how and why people behave as they do are similar to what personality psychologists do. When we talk about an individual's personality we are talking about the characteristic patterns of thoughts, feelings and behaviors that make a person unique. In addition, personality and style arises from within the individual and remains fairly consistent throughout life, with slight variations. For example, someone who is very extroverted is unlikely to become introverted as a result of experience, though they may on occasions have to display the opposite characteristic because of the demands or pressures of work. However, if they have to act outside of their normal style or preference for prolonged periods they may begin to exhibit signs of stress. This is why it is very important to analyse your style as it has implications for the sort of work you like doing and the sort of environment in which you are likely to feel comfortable.

Some of the fundamental characteristics of personality include:

- Consistency – behaviour is not as random as we might imagine; there is a recognisable order and regularity to how we behave. Essentially, people act in the same way or similar ways in a variety of situations.

- Psychological and Physiological Basis – personality has a psychological component and is also influenced by biological processes.

- Impacts behaviours and actions – personality causes us to act and behave in a certain way.

- Multiple expressions – personality can be seen in how we behave, what we think, how we feel and how we interact with people.

Within the occupational setting there are many different personality inventories available. Some of the more popular are OPP's Myers Briggs Type Indicator (MBTI) and 16PF, Saville Consulting Wave and SHL's OPQ32. All of these questionnaires are available on-line and require administration and interpretation by a qualified practitioner. The exercise on the following page is a self-administered, self-interpreted exercise, and although it is not a standardised personality questionnaire it will provide you with an insight into your own style and preferences to help you to identify your own special strengths. This understanding can give you an insight into what kinds of work you might enjoy and be successful doing.

Time: This exercise will take you about 20 minutes to complete.

Step 1

Take a look at the list of personality traits and characteristics. Circle those personality traits which best describe you. Try to be as honest as you can and not answer as you would like to be. Your first response is generally your best response; don't ponder any one question for too long.

Group 1 – Practical	Group 2 – Creative	Group 3 – Entrepreneurial
Rational	Imaginative	Ambitious
Practical	Intuitive	Risk Taker
Cautious	Inventive	Confident
Conventional	Original	Quick Minded
Pragmatic	Insightful	Persuasive
Methodical	Ingenious	Competitive
Reliable	Imaginatively Curious	Flexible
Industrious	Creative	Impulsive
Realistic	Enthusiastic	Energetic
Concrete	Complex	Resourceful
Sensible	Deep	Spontaneous
Systematic	Disorderly	Visionary
Routine	Innovative	Engaging
Consistent	Distracted	Enterprising
Technical	Expressive	Active
P_____	C_____	E_____

Group 4 – Social	Group 5 – Intellectual	Group 6 – Administrative
Patient	Analytical	Dominant
Sociable	Investigative	Structured
Empathetic	Intellectually Curious	Decisive
Generous	Critical	Efficient
Helpful	Challenging	Logical Problem Solver
Sensitive	Independent	Factual
Idealistic	Reserved	Competent
Dependable	Quiet	Tough
Cooperative	Logical	Clear
Emotional	Intelligent	Assertive
Loyal	Detached	Organised
Warm	Abstract Problem Solver	Strategic
Team Player	Incisive	Direct
Understanding	Skeptical	Fair
	Theoretical	Objective
S_____	I_____	A_____

Step 2

Score each circled or checked item as one point. Enter the total in the space below each column. Next determine which column has the highest score and which column has the next highest score. These columns are the ones which best reflect your own personality and style.

Step 3

Read the interpretation below for each of the different personalities and styles and determine which roles would best suit your particular personality and style.

Practical Column

If you scored highest on the Practical Column the following will generally be true of you:

- Value tradition and security
- Can be depended on to follow through on tasks
- Stable, practical and down to earth

- Dislike doing things which don't make sense
- Respect for facts and concrete information
- Appreciate structured and orderly environments
- Not naturally in-tune with other people's feelings
- Action -oriented "doers"
- Excellent trouble shooters, able to quickly find solutions to a wide variety of practical problems
- Hard working and dependable
- Generally don't like change; their motto is "if it ain't broke why fix it".
- Learn best "hands on".
- Interested in how and why things work
- Like to see immediate results for their actions
- Excellent memory for detail.

Individuals who have traits associated with the Practical Column are pragmatic and down to earth. They have a preference for working with the concrete and practical and like immediate results.

Possible career choices for the Practical Column are:

◊ Librarian
◊ Law Enforcement
◊ Accountant
◊ Carpenter
◊ Builder
◊ Engineering or science technician
◊ Mechanic
◊ Chef
◊ Auditor.

Creative Column

If you scored highest on the Creative Column the following will generally be true of you:

- Creative and inspirational
- Enjoy generating creative and imaginative ideas
- Enjoy variety and new challenges

- Complex and deep
- Original and individualistic – don't fall into the mainstream
- Prefer to work alone, and may have problems working on a team
- Dislike dealing with details and routine
- Excellent verbal and written communication skills
- Extremely intuitive and perceptive about life
- Well-developed appreciation for aesthetic beauty
- Likely to be original and unconventional
- Hate being confined to strict schedules and regimens
- Need space and freedom to do things their own way.

Individuals who have traits associated with the Creative Column are drawn towards careers and professions that allow them to express their creative talents and insights. They are complex and deep and are sometimes seen as distracted and difficult to understand.

Possible career choices for the Creative Column are:

◊ Writer or editor
◊ Artist or entertainer
◊ Architect
◊ Marketing professional
◊ Musician or composer
◊ Interior designer
◊ Photographer
◊ Teacher in the arts.

Entrepreneurial Column

If you scored highest on the Entrepreneurial Column the following will generally be true of you:

- Action-oriented
- Fast-paced and energetic
- Flexible and adaptable
- Resourceful
- Attracted to adventure and risk
- Like initiating things but not necessarily following through

- Creative and ingenious
- Bright and capable
- Great motivators of people
- Visionaries
- Natural leaders
- Excellent communication skills
- Enjoy generating ideas
- Dislike confining schedules and environments.

Individuals who have traits associated with the Entrepreneurial Column are outgoing and action-oriented. They are quick to spot opportunities and tend to live in the future of possibilities.

Possible career choices for the Entrepreneurial Column are:

◊ Public relations
◊ Marketing executive
◊ Business development
◊ Consultant
◊ Sales
◊ Corporate executive.

Social Column

If you scored highest on the Social Column the following will generally be true of you:

- Strong value systems
- Warmly interested in people
- Service-oriented, usually putting the needs of others above their own
- Loyal and devoted to people and causes
- Strong people skills
- Sensitive and compassionate to people
- Highly principled
- Value people's feelings
- Get personal satisfaction from helping others
- Value harmony and are uncomfortable with conflict
- Work well in a team environment – cooperative and friendly
- Need approval from others.

Individuals who have traits associated with the Social Column are naturally people oriented. They enjoy working with people and using their people skills in a caring capacity. They are good team players being naturally co-operative and helpful and will look to bring harmony to any situation they work in.

Possible career choices for the Social Column are:

◊ Counsellor/social worker

◊ Teacher/professor

◊ Psychologist

◊ Psychiatrist

◊ Human resources manager

◊ Facilitator

◊ Medical/nursing

◊ Waitress/waiter

◊ Child care worker.

Intellectual Column

If you scored highest on the Intellectual Column the following will generally be true of you:

* Good at working with complex theories and concepts

* Enjoy the world of ideas and concepts – may not always be practical

* Value originality

* Become bored easily

* Can concentrate for long periods of time

* Future oriented and strong strategist

* Reserved and detached from others

* Look to solve difficult challenging theories

* Strong insights and intuitions

* Have very high standards of performance

* Very logical and rational

* Independent and original – will resist strongly being controlled.

Individuals who have traits associated with the Intellectual Column are insightful and intuitive when it comes to seeing the bigger picture. They tend to live in the future and look for mental stimulation. They become bored easily and are always seeking new and complex challenges. They can work for long periods on complex ideas.

Possible career choices for the Intellectual Column are:

◊ Writer

◊ Scientist

◊ IT professional

◊ Solicitor/Barrister

◊ Researcher

◊ Management consultant

◊ Engineer

◊ Strategic planner

◊ University lecturer/professor.

Administrative Column

If you scored highest on the Administrative Column the following will generally be true of you:

• Natural born leaders

• Like to be in control and take charge

• Are comfortable working in large organisations where they can use their organisational skills

• Won't shy away from making hard decisions

• Treat people fairly but may not always be sympathetic or understanding

• Well developed strategic brains

• Impatient with inefficiency and incompetence

• Excellent communication skills

• Self-confident

• Can be relied on in a crisis.

Individuals who have traits associated with the Administrative Column have strong organisational skills. They love structure and order and are very comfortable in a leadership role. They have a clear set of beliefs and standards which they live by. They are good trouble shooters and problem solvers.

Possible career choices for the Administrative Column are:

◊ Business executive

◊ Accountant and financial director

◊ Management consultant

◊ Banker

◊ Engineer
◊ Business strategist.

Step 4

Based on the above descriptions are there any trends that you see coming through? How does what you are currently doing reflect your own personality and style? What changes might you need to make, if any?

_____

_____

_____

_____

_____

_____

_____

CLARIFYING YOUR VALUES

Your values, what you care about, guide your actions and determine how you experience different aspects of the world. Whenever you say that something is important to you or has significance for you, you are stating a value. Think of things you have or would like to have, such as a new house, or a vintage car, or a new computer. Things have qualities about them that we value. Think of characteristics you admire in people – like courage, loyalty, honour, love, self-control. Think of conditions in life that you desire, such as prosperity, success, abundance, good health, beauty and confidence. All of these are values.

Values are not static. They change and evolve over time to reflect new experiences and new stages in your life and career. As a child, for example, your most important value may have been winning the love and approval of your parents. As you grow and mature, new values, such as autonomy, achievement and the need for self-approval, may come to the fore. Parenthood may shift the emphasis once again to nurturance, family and achieving financial stability.

It is all too easy, however, to lose touch with what is important to you in the process of managing your day-to-day activities and tasks. Moreover, because you rarely stop to reflect on your values, you may fail to "catch-up" with changes in how you see the world. Understanding your values can help you in:

• Determining personal and career goals

• Making decisions about your career and personal life

- Selecting the kind of position and working environment which best matches your own needs and preferences
- Understanding the kind of people you most like to associate with
- Allocating your money and time to achieve the greatest personal satisfaction.

The following activities will help you to develop greater awareness of what is most important to you, and what you want out of your life and your career.

Time: These exercises will take you about 45 minutes to complete.

EXERCISE 1: VALUES CLARIFICATION

Step One

For some it can be difficult to identify what your true values are, particularly if like most people your days are a juggling act between children, family, work and home life. The following sentence completion activity is a great way to get you thinking about what you truly value and is a helpful precursor to the values exercises that follow.

If I won the lotto I would _____

What I would wish to change in this world is _____

What I want most in my life is _____

The greatest joy in my life is _____

If I had 24 hours to live I would _____

The people I work best with are _____

The types of work environments I enjoy most are _____

The advice I would give my children is _____

Step Two

Having completed the exercise, look at the sentences and pick out those words which you believe best reflect the values that hold true for you, both from a personal and a work perspective. Use these words as a framework to help you complete the following exercise.

Step Three

In the spaces below, list up to ten key values from the exercise which you have identified, in the order which you feel are most important.

1.	6.
2.	7.
3.	8.
4.	9.
5.	10.

EXERCISE 2: PERSONAL VALUES EXERCISE

Step One

Read the list of 20 personal values below (this is by no means a definitive list; add any which you feel are missing) and tick those which are important to you. Having identified those which are important, rank them from the most important value to the least important value.

Alternatively, if it is feasible print the names of the values on small cards. Add any important values you feel are missing. Then do a card sort exercise as follows.

Sort 1: Sort the values which are most important to you, and those which are not as important to you. Try to assign roughly half to each category.

Sort 2: Take those cards which are most important to you and rank them from the most to the least important values.

Personal Values	NB	Rank
Aesthetics To appreciate and enjoy beautiful things and works of art		
Altruism To have regard or devotion to the interests of others		
Affiliation To be accepted and liked by others; to work closely with others; to belong		
Companionship To obtain and share warmth, caring, companionship with family, friends or co-workers		
Creativity To create new and innovative ideas and designs		
Emotional Well-Being Having peace of mind and inner security, free of anxiety and barriers to effective functioning		
Family To spend time with my family or meaningful others; to build strong relationships with those who are important to me and to spend quality time with them		
Growth To develop to my full potential to become a better and more rounded person; to be constantly learning, changing and developing		
Health To be physically fit and healthy		
Integrity To act in terms of my convictions; to be honest; to stand up for my beliefs		

Personal Values	NB	Rank
Justice To have fair treatment of others; exhibit fairness and righteousness		
Location To live where I want to live		
Love To have a loving attachment to another		
Loyalty Having a connection to a person, group or community		
Pleasure To have fun; to enjoy my life and my work		
Privacy To respect one's privacy and that of others		
Respect and Dignity for Self and Others To demonstrate respect and dignity for myself and for other people; to hold myself and others in high regard		
Spiritual Well Being To have inner harmony; to be at peace with myself; to live by my beliefs		
Wealth To have abundance of valuable material possessions and affluence		
Wisdom To have insight at the highest level; to be able to discern inner qualities and relationships		
Other		

Step Two

Write your top five personal values in the spaces below:

1._____

2._____

3._____

4._____

5._____

EXERCISE 3: WORK VALUES EXERCISE

Now let's have a look at your work values. This exercise is basically the same as the one for your personal values.

Step One

Read the list of 20 work values below (this is by no means a definitive list; add any which you feel are missing) and tick those which are important to you. Having identified those which are important, rank them from the most important value to the least important value.

Alternatively, if it is feasible print the names of the values on small cards. Add any important values you feel are missing. Then do a card sort exercise as follows.

Sort 1: Sort the values which are most important to you, and those which are not as important to you. Try to assign roughly half to each category.

Sort 2: Take those cards which are most important to you and rank them from the most to the least important values.

Personal Values	NB	Rank
Achievement To accomplish important things; to reach the top of my area of professionalism or organisation		
Advancement To have the opportunity to be promoted; to move to a higher level job		
Autonomy To be able to establish and act in terms of my own priorities and time schedule; to be free of organisational rules and norms		
Challenge To be involved in interesting, challenging work		
Competence To be respected for my competence; to have my worth recognised by others		
Expertise To become a known and respected authority in what I do; to achieve excellence in my work		
Development Opportunities To learn new skills; to have opportunity to develop and grow in the role		
Financial Freedom To be financially successful; to earn good money		
Flexible Working To have a flexible work schedule; to be able to determine my own hours and work input		
Friendship To develop friendly relationships and companionship in work		

Personal Values	NB	Rank
Leadership To exert influence; to direct the efforts of others		
Intellectual Stimulation To have challenging, stimulating work which stretches me mentally		
Pleasure/Fun To have a chance to play at work and have fun; enjoy what I am doing		
Power To have control, authority and influence over others		
Recognition To have status; to be made to feel significant and important; to earn the respect and recognition of others		
Security To achieve a secure and stable work and financial situation		
Service To help other people; to feel that I am making a contribution to the well-being of others; to help improve society		
Tangible Results To have the satisfaction of seeing what has been produced		
Teamwork To work with other people as part of a team; people who are easy to get along with		
Variety To have different activities, problems, people, rather than a fixed routine		
Other		

Step Two

Write your top five work values in the spaces below:

1._____

2._____

3._____

4._____

5._____

EXERCISE FOUR: SUMMARY OF YOUR MOST IMPORTANT VALUES

Step One

Copy your personal and work values listed as high importance into the first column of the Value Assessor (next page). Study each of these values in turn. For each value, ask yourself such questions as:

• How would I feel if this value was satisfied much more or much less than it is now?

• How important is this value compared to other values I have rated as being of high importance to me?

Step Two

Column II: Evaluate the importance of each value to you by assigning it a score out of 10 points. Give a rating of 10 to the value that is most important to you of all. Assign ratings of less than 10 to reflect the relative importance of the remaining values, for example, give a score of 5 to a value that is only half as important as your most important value.

Step Three

Now you have an approximate standard for evaluating your experiences. For each value you have listed, ask yourself the following:

• Considering all aspects of my work how well am I satisfying this particular value?

• Considering all aspects of my personal life, how well am I satisfying this particular value?

Step Four

Record your judgments in the final columns. Let 10 represent "absolute and complete satisfaction, no need for improvement". Let 5 represent "moderate satisfaction" and 0 "no satisfaction at all". Use other numbers between 0 and 10 as appropriate.

Value Assessor – Summary Table of Your Most Important Values

Important Values	Importance Rating	Value Satisfaction in Work	Value Satisfaction in Personal Life
1.			
2.			
3.			
4.			
5.			
6.			
7.			
8.			
9.			
10.			

Summary of Values

In descending order my most important values are:

1. _____

2. _____

3. _____

4. _____

5. _____

My values which are being satisfied in my present position are:

_____

_____

_____

_____

_____

My values which are not currently being satisfied are:

_____

_____

_____

_____

_____

Some ways in which I may be able to achieve greater satisfaction of my values in my work life include (brainstorm):

_____

_____

_____

_____

_____

Some ways in which I may be able to achieve greater satisfaction of my values in my personal lift include (brainstorm):

_____

_____

_____

_____

_____

_____

_____

LIFESTYLE SATISFACTION ASSESSMENT

Career planning and personal development should never take place in isolation. The decisions you make about these areas can have a major impact on your life outside work, just as your activities outside work can have considerable impact on your career and personal development.

For example, if you are considering a career change, it may be necessary for you to go back to college or university and give up a significant portion of your leisure time. Similarly, while business travel is a normal part of organisational life, some job assignments require more travel than others. In considering a new assignment you may want to determine how much travel is involved, and what effect that will have on your personal and family life.

At the same time, it may be necessary to make certain trade-offs between career and personal development. Only you can decide exactly what trade-offs you are prepared to make.

In any event, no matter how challenging and satisfying your work life, it cannot meet all of your needs for personal growth and development. You have, or ought to have, a rewarding life outside work as well and a narrow concentration on your job is by no means a guarantee of ultimate career success. Indeed, successful people are usually well-balanced, with a number of outside interests. Rather than detracting from their career success, a full leisure and family life refreshes them to perform more effectively at work, and allows them to bring a broader scope of vision to their jobs.

The next activity asks you to review how well you are currently balancing the different areas of your lift, and to develop goals and action plans to address identified areas of weakness.

Time: This exercise will take you about 30 minutes to complete.

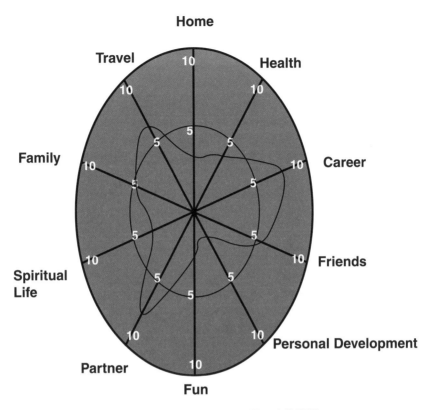

Figure 2: Life Satisfaction Wheel (LSW)

Introduction

To be fulfilled it is important to try to live a balanced life. The Lifestyle Satisfaction Wheel (LSW) provides you with a pictorial overview as to how well the important areas of your life are currently balanced. It is all too easy to find yourself out of kilter with what is important to you as the demands of life become even more pressing. So, by using the LSW periodically, you will be in a better position to judge whether you are creating the right balance in your life and ultimately getting the most satisfaction from your life that you can. Use the LSW to check your current level of satisfaction or fulfilment by assessing how much time and attention you are giving to each area. The centre of the wheel represents one (low) and the outer edge represents ten (high). As you check your current level of satisfaction using the LSW as a guide, you will notice that it is quite up and down and it will bring into focus those areas that you need to change. As you examine the LSW, decide where you want to take action. Figure 2 above shows an example of a LSW with example areas. Below is a guide as to how you can create your own LSW.

Step 1

From the list below pick out 12 areas that are important to you right now and represent the different dimensions of your life. If there is a dimension that is important to you but is not captured in the categories below add it in. You may wish to add some of the values that you identified as important in the values exercise. Alternatively, you may find that the list of dimensions in the different categories are not specific enough. For example, rather than having physical fitness as a category you may want to capture the activity you enjoy which keeps you physically fit, like running, walking or dancing. Or you may want to list some of your hobbies such as gardening, painting, learning an instrument, etc. Use this instrument in the way that best works for you.

Physical/ Tangibles	Emotional	Spiritual	Mental	Social
Health Physical Fitness Financial Travel Physical Appearance Home Possessions	Fun Recreation Social Life Emotional Well-being Love	Spiritual Life Nature Religion Inner Growth	Attitude Career Education Work Personal Development	Family Partner/ Marriage Children Friends Community Hobbies

Step 2

On the LSW Worksheet on the following page, list your dimensions or areas on the 12 spokes of the wheel. Assign a rating to each on a scale of 1 to 10 in terms of the amount of time and attention you are giving to it, and hence your level of satisfaction, with 1 being low and 10 being high. Once you have done this for each dimension you should link each area until it forms a circle. This will give you an overview of how well your life is balanced. A balanced life does not mean getting a 10 in each area. There are times when some areas need more attention than others and that means that you will have to make compromises. The LSW is about trying to create balance and perspective in those areas most important to you.

Step 3

Now think about your ideal level in each area; create a second circle using a different colour to represent your ideal. You should now see where the gaps are and the areas that you would like to work on. Ask yourself:

Am I satisfied with how I am currently balancing my life?

What parts of my lift seem out of balance?

What is the impact of this neglect on me, and on other important people in my life?

What activities am I spending too much time and/or energy on, and what can I do about it?

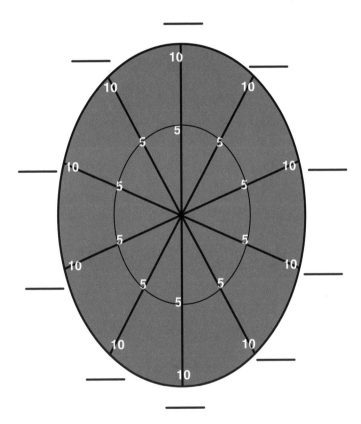

Figure 3: Life Satisfaction Wheel (LSW) Worksheet

Step 4

Now take two or three areas that you want to start working on. In the left hand column on the following page, write your goals, for example, "I want to spend more time on physical fitness". In the right hand column state what you intend to do about this goal, for example, "lose weight; go to the gym three times a week".

You should revisit your goals on a frequent basis to remind yourself what you want from life and check that you are working towards these goals and desires. You should also write down the things you want to stop doing because they are preventing you from feeling really satisfied, as well as the things you want to continue doing. Be specific as to how you are going to achieve both of these things.

Goals	Action Plan (What I'm going to do about this)
I want to start:	
I want to stop:	
I want to continue:	

4

Exploring Your Career

• •

"You are the embodiment of the information you choose to accept and act upon. To change your circumstances you need to change your thinking and subsequent actions." – Aldin Sinclair

• •

INTRODUCTION

You will most likely change careers several times during your life. How successful you'll be in making those transitions can at least be partially attributed to the amount of career planning and preparation you've done. Taking a retrospective look at what you have found fulfilling, and what works and doesn't work for you in a job, is an important first step in this planning and preparation. Knowing your unique selling points gives you a head start in selling yourself either in your current job or in the job market.

Tom Peters advocates that individuals must take a systematic approach to marketing and selling themselves to potential employers. Individuals, like organisations, should constantly reinvent themselves to ensure that they are attractive "products" in the labour market. They should identify and develop their brand, and then take the necessary steps to build and maintain that brand.

This section will help you to begin that process. It builds on the previous section by exploring the skills you have developed through education, jobs, hobbies, volunteer work, clubs and the like. It also gives you the opportunity to further explore what is really important to you in your career in terms of the people you work with, the manager or supervisor who will get the best from you, the types of companies that are most appealing and the sort of skills you want to use and develop.

The tools in this chapter will help you:

- Identify sources of satisfaction and dissatisfaction in your job
- Take stock of your career to date, identifying the highs and lows, and looking ahead to be clear about what you want from the future.

Identifying Sources of Satisfaction and Dissatisfaction in Your Job

It is rare for someone to be completely satisfied or dissatisfied with a particular job. Typically, we like some aspects of our work while disliking others, to a greater or lesser degree. This exercise will help you accurately evaluate and clarify your feelings about the individual components of your job. It will help clarify areas which you may need to minimise in your current job where possible, and it will provide important information about your career preferences.

If on the whole you like your job, it is important to pinpoint precisely what it is you like about it so that you can seek out those same underlying job features in the future, while minimising the things you do not like as much as possible.

If you are dissatisfied with your current position, this analysis will be all the more important. It may be, on reflection, that your dissatisfaction is with only one or two aspects which have come to assume a disproportionately negative significance. For example, a person whose job involves chairing meetings and giving presentations, and who dislikes those activities, may become extremely dissatisfied or unhappy with their job, even though there are many other aspects of it that they actually enjoy.

In completing this exercise you will:

- Begin to develop specifications and action plans for possibly modifying your present position to build in more of what you want and to reduce aspects you find less satisfying.
- Develop guidelines and criteria for evaluating future career moves.

Time: This exercise will take you 30–45 minutes to complete.

Instructions

Below you will find a number of potential sources of job dissatisfaction – potential because what you may find annoying may be a source of satisfaction to someone else. This is not intended as a complete list – its purpose is to stimulate your thinking.

Read through the list and tick off the items that describe how you feel about your present position. Even if you are not currently in a job you can still do this exercise to help clarify what would provide you with the greatest source of satisfaction in any future job. Add any other items that occur to you in the space provided.

Exploring Your Career

Possible Job Dissatisfiers	Tick Applicable Box
Not having enough flexibility in your work activities	
No personal or developmental growth opportunities in the job	
Too much bureaucracy and red tape	
Poorly rewarded or recognised for hard work	
No opportunity to manage or direct others	
Lack of team work; team members too political or unfriendly	
Hours are too long	
Not enough recognition for your contribution	
Lack of clarity about what is expected of you in the job	
Difficulty getting on with your immediate supervisor or manager	
Unable to control the pace of your work – either too fast or too slow	
Lack of job security and a sense of belonging	
Pay is inadequate	
Lack of job promotion prospects	
Too much or not enough travel	
Not enough challenge in the job to really motivate you	
Too much control over how you do your work	

Possible Job Dissatisfiers	Tick Applicable Box
Not enough feedback on how well or poorly you are performing in the role	
Few opportunities to socialise or interact with colleagues	
Too much time spent working as part of a team	
Lack of variety in your work and role	
No opportunity to exercise your own professionalism or develop your expertise	
Little opportunity to exercise leadership or to influence others	
Too much control and not enough flexibility generally (determine how, when, where you will work	
Other:	

Instructions

Copy your own list of dissatisfiers onto the first column of a new page. In the second column write what you want in your job. Be as specific as possible. Do not censor your ideas. Write down what you would ideally want in light of the things dissatisfying you. Some dissatisfiers you may be able to eliminate but others you won't. Be creative in thinking about how you might be able to turn these dissatisfiers around to your benefit and something positive.

Here is an example:

Things Dissatisfying Me at Work	What I Want in My Job
Lack of variety in my work or role	Opportunity to work on projects outside my normal work and to work in other departments for short periods
Not enough travel	Opportunity to travel to our offices in Europe and US at least twice a year
Lack of flexibility in the role	Spend two days a week working from home and work the flexi time system in terms of hours
Lack of clarify as to what is expected	Clearly defined goals and objectives
Always working in groups and teams	Opportunity to work alone
No personal development opportunities	Opportunity to work in or with another department (marketing?)

Things Dissatisfying Me at Work	What I Want in My Job

Now you will repeat the preceding three steps for the things you find satisfying about your job.

Read through the list and tick those items that describe how you feel about your position. Add any other items that occur to you in the space provided.

Possible Job Satisfiers	Tick Applicable Box
High visibility in the role	
Lots of interesting and varied work	
Opportunity to meet new people	
Colleagues who are supportive and friendly	
A supervisor/manager who is encouraging and supportive	
Working environment is pleasant and has plenty of amenities (e.g. canteen, gym)	
Lots of interesting social activities organised	
Considered to be a valued employee	
Good benefits and remuneration	
Plenty of personal development and growth opportunities	
Good promotion prospects	
Flexible working arrangements	
Good family friendly policies and child care benefits	
Supportive and friendly work environment	
A progressive company which provides challenge and opportunity	

Possible Job Satisfiers	Tick Applicable Box
Work usually done in teams	
Plenty of opportunities to develop my technical expertise	
Have control over how I do my work	
Very clear guidelines as to what is expected	
High profile organisation	
Believe in the product/services	
Opportunities to lead and influence the direction of the business	
Leadership and management responsibilities	
Others	

Instructions

Now copy your list of satisfiers onto the first column on the next page. In the second column note the things you want to maintain and/or have more of in your current and future jobs. Again, do not worry for the moment how realistic these ideas are.

Here is an example:

What I Like About My Current Job	Things I Want to Maintain and/or Have More of in Current and Future Assignments
Opportunity to meet new people	Working with outside clients and building my profile externally
Promotion prospects	To move up two levels in the next five years. Or to build my reputation through hosting an art exhibition in London.
Personal growth and opportunity	To attend next years HR conference in the UK. To host a community event to support people who are unemployed.
High visibility in the work I do	Take up secondment opportunities in our European offices
A lot of teamwork in my department	More opportunity to work with other departments in a teamwork environment
Working with people I can learn from	Working with Dave; learning a lot about management from him
High pressure environment	Working under pressure to meet deadlines

What I Like About My Current Job	Things I Want to Maintain and/or Have More of in Current and Future Assignments

Instructions

1. Examine the lists you have made in the right-hand column of your two tables. Highlight in yellow the items on these lists that are most important to you. Few jobs are absolutely perfect, and you almost always have to make certain trade-offs. When you set clear priorities for yourself you will be much better able to determine what trade-offs you are prepared to make. You will be able to discuss the issues that are really important to you with your manager, and may be able to modify your current job to better suit your needs. You will also be able to make more informed choices in thinking about future jobs or roles, and about the types of work settings in which you will be most effective and productive.

2. Summary and Action Plan: Now begin to think about how you can get what you want. First, think of some realistic ideas for improving your current job to form a basis for eventual discussion with your employer or manager. Then write some specifications for your next job, focusing on possible jobs or assignments which match with what you want.

Summary and Action Plan

Some ways in which I can improve my present job are:

_____

_____

_____

_____

In my next job I want:

_____

_____

_____

_____

In my next job I don't want:

_____

_____

_____

_____

Some possible jobs/assignments which match with what I want are (brainstorm):

_____

_____

_____

_____

CAREER HISTORY ANALYSIS

In the preceding exercise you conducted a fairly detailed analysis of the components of your present job and identified specific job "likes" and "dislikes".

How you feel about your current position tells only part of the story. It is also important to analyse the positions you have held in the past and to draw the connections between where you have been and where you are now. That, in turn, will provide valuable information for deciding what is important to you and where you want to go in the future.

Exploring Your Career

In completing this exercise, you will be conducting an analysis of your career history in order to increase your understanding and knowledge of:

* How your past positions have contributed to your development
* The skills and abilities you have acquired over your career
* Underlying career orientations and preferences.

This exercise is for individuals who have held two or more positions/jobs.

Time: This exercise will take you 30–45 minutes to complete.

Past, Present, Future Enjoyed

In the box below put ten words in each box to describe what you enjoyed about work you did in the past, what you enjoy doing now and what you want to be doing in the future.

Past	Present	Future

Past, Present, Future Not Enjoyed

Now put ten words in each box in the box below to describe what you did not enjoy about work you did in the past, you don't enjoy doing now and don't want to be doing in the future.

Past	Present	Future

Past, Present, Future Skills/Knowledge/Abilities You Acquired and Enjoyed

Next put ten words in each box in the box below to describe what skills/knowledge/abilities you acquired and enjoyed in the past, you are using now and want to be using in the future.

Past	Present	Future

Summary of Career Themes

Review your worksheets for this and the preceding exercise and look for any re-peating patterns or themes. Complete the following sentences:

In analysing my career history, it appears that I am most happy when:

_____

_____

_____

_____

_____

_____

_____

I am least satisfied when:

_____

_____

_____

_____

_____

_____

_____

In these roles/positions I acquired the following key skills, knowledge, abilities:

_____

_____

_____

_____

_____

_____

_____

5

Exploring Your Dream Career

LOOKING TO THE FUTURE: WHAT DO YOU WANT?

You have conducted a thorough assessment of your interests, skills, values, work style and preferences. Now it is time to put this information together. The purpose of this exercise is to summarise key information about yourself which will help determine your career target and to identify some possible career goals for achieving that target. Then you will be ready to move on to Section Three which is all about assessing your key strengths and development needs against the qualities and skills that matter in a career and developing action plans to enhance your talents and minimize your weaknesses.

YOUR DREAM CAREER

Based on what you have learned about yourself consider your ideal job. Don't worry about being overly realistic. (This is a fantasy exercise.) If you can think of more than one ideal job, list these as well. If you can't think of anything then try answering the following question: "If you could be anything you wanted, what would you be?" If you can't think of any possible job titles, then try to identify possible roles or functions. In thinking about your ideal job you should consider the following options.

- **Similar role** to what you are currently doing perhaps in a different organisation or working in a different country or industry sector

- **Job enrichment** – carrying out similar tasks but adding more complexity. Consider, for example, participating in or chairing a task force; working with someone from whom you can learn, delegating some of your responsibilities to free yourself for other work which challenges you
- **Promotion** – looking to enhance what you are doing at a more senior level
- **Lateral move** – moving into a new department or area to enhance your skill base. This could include moving from Finance into HR, for example.
- **Step down** – moving down a level where you decide to take on less responsibility
- **New area completely** – you may decide that you want to leave what you are currently doing and go into something completely different, for example, leaving your finance job and pursuing graphic design
- **Different industry sector** – using your competencies in a different industry sector
- **Setting up your own business** – develop a customer/client base where you can sell your services independently
- **Contractual work** – where you work for different organisations on a contract basis for set periods of time.

1. My ideal job is:

_____

_____

_____

_____

_____

_____

_____

_____

Now complete the following questions in terms of your ideal job. If you couldn't identify any ideal jobs, then answer the questions in terms of your ideal job characteristics, roles or functions.

2. What skills would you be using?

_____

_____

_____

_____

_____

_____

_____

_____

3. What kinds of people would you be interacting with? (for example, very bright, fun to be with, powerful, senior management, professional, organised, supportive, etc.)

_____

_____

_____

_____

_____

_____

_____

_____

4. What would be the special features of your working environment? (for example, task-oriented, people-oriented, a lot of autonomy, a lot of variety, etc.) What would be the scope of your responsibility?

_____

_____

_____

_____

_____

_____

_____

5. What would the relationship with your manager be like? What qualities will they possess and how would you like them to interact with you? (for example, focused, supportive, give you lots of scope to do your own thing, etc.)

_____

_____

_____

_____

_____

_____

_____

6. What kind of roles or functions would you be playing? (for example, managing, giving technical advice, helping others, etc.)

_____

_____

_____

_____

_____

_____

7. Which of your important values would you be satisfying?

_____

_____

_____

_____

_____

_____

Your Career Target

Based on your previous analysis, fill out the table on the following page. This can be used to focus your job search, to communicate your needs and requirements and to benchmark potential jobs.

Ideal Job	
Skills being used	
Nature of people interaction	
Features of work environment	
Management style	
Scope of responsibility	
Roles or function	
Values being fulfilled	
Location	

Action Plan

1. Do you know of any positions or types of positions within your current role or within your organisation which might match your responses to the above? List them.

_____

_____

_____

_____

_____

_____

_____

2. What kind of special training or development do you think you would need to fulfill this job successfully?

_____

_____

_____

_____

_____

_____

_____

3. What actions can you take to begin moving towards your career target and what companies might you research that could provide those opportunities? (for example, talk to people who currently work in those areas that are of interest; begin to develop the necessary qualifications and skills to perform for that role, etc.)

_____

_____

_____

_____

_____

_____

_____

Part Three

Taking Stock of Your Work Effectiveness and Development Planning

Assessing Your Work Style Effectiveness

Reality Testing

Development Options

6

Assessing Your Work Style Effectiveness

INTRODUCTION

With downsizing becoming more prevalent and a depression in the job market, it is becoming even more critical that you know what is expected of you and that you have the necessary qualities to perform to the highest level. One of the questions you should be asking yourself in today's climate is how you can get the competitive edge that is going to make a difference to how you perform in any current or future roles you may aspire to? Knowing what is critical in the role you hold or aspire to is an important first step. But to be truly successful you must utilise your strengths to best effect and minimise as much as possible your development needs. However, this needs to be done in a planned and meaningful way and against the backdrop of what makes for superior performance.

WORK STYLE EFFECTIVENESS MODEL (WSEM)

Research has clearly shown that once you have reached a proficient level necessary to perform effectively in your role, the qualities that set superior performers apart from their average counterparts are ones associated with emotional and social intelligence. The Work Style Effectiveness Model (WSEM), of which there are sixteen dimensions, combines the most important skills and qualities that matter in a career and covers a number of dimensions associated with emotional and social intelligence. It is based on extensive experience as to the factors that make for superior performance and pulls together the best of what career experts have to say on this topic. It works on the principle that those who outperform their peers are those who excel in these areas.

This section will enable you to assess your strengths and development needs regarding important qualities and skills that matter in a career as captured in the WSEM, and to increase your self-awareness, which is the cornerstone of development. Following your assessment and analysis of your strengths and development needs you will be in a position to incorporate meaningful information into a development plan so that you can maximise your effectiveness and minimise your development needs.

The first step in this process is to take the WSEM questionnaire to analyse your effectiveness and establish your strengths and development needs. By completing the questionnaire you will get a fairer assessment of your effectiveness in each of the sixteen areas and allow you to compile your "personal profile".

As this is a generic model, not all of the sixteen areas will necessarily be important for your current role or the one you aspire to. Therefore, you will need to develop a "job profile" which incorporates the most important criteria for your current or future role. You can then match your "personal profile" with your "job profile" and put together a development action plan.

Following this analysis there is a development section which provides a sample of the kinds of activities that you can take to develop in several of the sixteen areas. In the Further Reading section at the back there is also a list of web resources and books which will give you more in-depth information on all sixteen development areas.

Developing Your Personal Profile Using the WSEM Questionnaire

The WSEM questionnaire will help you explore some important aspects of your work style effectiveness. Gaining increased awareness of where you are effective will help you to build on these areas and use them to best effect. Knowing your strengths can also help you in charting your career direction, and in identifying the jobs in which you will be most satisfied and productive. At the same time, it is important to know in which areas you might need development, particularly if these are critical to job success. Your results will help you answer such questions as:

- What are the distinctive characteristics of your own work style?

- What are your particular strengths and how can you utilise these more effectively?

- What elements of your work style might you want to modify in order to realise your full potential?

Instructions for Completing the WSEM Questionnaire:

For each of the statements in the questionnaire, select the number on the scale which most closely characterises your personal feelings. Write the number in the space provided beside the statement. There are no right or wrong answers and it is important that you are as honest as possible.

Use the full range of the scale. If you always answer a "3" or "4" you will not be able to derive maximum benefit from this questionnaire, so please be as honest as you can as this exercise is for your benefit.

As you complete this questionnaire, you may feel that some of the items seem repetitive. In fact, each statement is different. Therefore, it is important that you treat each statement as a new item.

After you have completed the questionnaire, you will be able to interpret your answers using the attached self-interpretation guide.

Time: This exercise will take about two hours to complete.

HOW CHARACTERISTIC IS THIS STATEMENT OF YOU?

1 .... 2 .... 3 .... 4 .... 5 6
Not at all   Extremely

Characteristic	Score
1. Anticipates and plans for future events	
2. Generates new and imaginative ideas	
3. Distinguishes between relevant and irrelevant information	
4. Has a sound knowledge of their area of expertise	
5. Sets clear goals and targets	
6. Makes things happen	
7. Leads from a place of passion and belief	
8. Is able to present ideas clearly and succinctly	
9. Is open to new ways of doing things	
10. Develops and builds positive relationships	
11. Actively participates and engages in collaborative team working projects	
12. Recovers quickly from setbacks	
13. Has a well developed sense of self and others	
14. Has a clear sense of purpose and direction	
15. Tries to overcome obstacles, doesn't give up easily	

Characteristic	Score
16. Has the courage to stand by their convictions	
17. Willing to invest in their own development	
18. Simplifies problems that seem overwhelmingly complex	
19. Shows curiosity regarding new approaches in own area of expertise	
20. Is committed to achieving and maintaining high quality results	
21. Seizes opportunities and acts upon them	
22. Able to inspire action in others because of their passion and belief	
23. Communicates in a way which engages others	
24. Collaborates with others and builds mutually beneficial partnerships	
25. Makes time for long range planning	
26. Comes up with innovative solutions	
27. Genuinely values others' input and expertise	
28. Believes in a positive outcome	
29. Can accurately interpret their own feelings and can channel these to best effect	
30. Keeps perspective and holds on to key priorities in the face of challenges or distractions	
31. Is willing to stand by their values and what they believe in even if it is unpopular	

Characteristic	Score
32. Seeks feedback on own performance in order to enhance their effectiveness	
33. Ensures goals and plans are linked to a wider vision and strategy	
34. Not afraid to act in new and different ways to achieve a better outcome	
35. Aims to do each task better than before, e.g. more efficiently, more quickly, etc.	
36. Can juggle different priorities effectively	
37. Gets things done through others	
38. Convinces other people and reaches agreement on ideas, plans and activities	
39. Interacts with others in a way that builds respect and fosters trust	
40. Is a good team player; does their share of the work	
41. Recognises the interdependence between related actions	
42. Enjoys brainstorming and blue sky thinking	
43. Applies their skills and/or knowleddge in their area of expertise	
44. Maintains motivation and deals with frustration when things don't go according to plan channelling energy into something more positive	
45. Is aware of the impact of their own behaviour on others	
46. Makes suggestions or brings new ideas without them being solicited	
47. Presents with a self-assured confidence; has presence	

Characteristic	Score
48. Willing to share experiences and lessons learned with others	
49. Takes account of the broader impact of actions initiated	
50. Can think outside the box and come up with new ideas	
51. Is accepted by others as having a good deal of knowledge/skill in their area of expertise	
52. Not afraid to take the lead when the situation requires it	
53. Can present views effectively and negotiate mutually acceptable solutions	
54. Quickly builds rapport and puts others at ease	
55. Is able to relate to people at all levels and comfortable in most social situations	
56. Encourages people to participate as part of the team. notices people who appear to be 'left out' and actively seeks to involve them	
57. Takes a broad range of issues or factors into account when developing plans	
58. Is comfortable in an environment that encourages creative thinking and innovation	
59. Takes steps to maintain a deep understanding of their area of expertise	
60. Has a number of projects on the go	
61. Changes others' views and influences their decisions	
62. Builds a network of effective relationships with others	
63. Proactively shares information across teams	

Characteristic	Score
64. Tries to create a positive environment wherever they go	
65. Imagines future possibilities; operates from a "big picture" perspective	
66. Applies innovative solutions to make improvements	
67. Invests in their area of expertise	
68. Is energetic and enthusiastic	
69. Leadership is sincere; they live their values	
70. Reads relationships well, picking up subtle positive and negative signals	
71. Sees projects or tasks through to completion	
72. Can voice views that are unpopular and go out on a limb	
73. Challenges the status quo in order to make improvements	
74. Enjoys coming up with new solutions	
75. Used by others as a resource in their area of expertise	
76. Motivates others to act through their drive and energy	
77. Is seen as a mover/shaker	
78. Supports others in developing and releasing their potential	
79. Open to new perspectives and learning	
80. Acts to promote good working relationships regardless of personal likes or dislikes	

Characteristic	Score
81. Can cope with changing circumstances	
82. Finds original connections and patterns that others overlook	
83. Has a thorough grasp of relevant products and services in their area of expertise	
84. Stays close to the action	
85. Has a clear vision of where they are going	
86. Sees relationships as long term – working towards a level of trust and understanding	
87. Draws on a range of coping mechanisms to help maintain a positive attitude	
88. Builds time for self-reflection and learns from their experiences	
89. Is comfortable with the ambiguity that change presents	
90. Provides solutions to problems	
91. Measures the attainment of outcomes	
92. Generates commitment and trust in others	
93. Does not pursue their own status or gain at the expense of others	
94. Able to persist and stay focused on the task at hand	
95. "Owns" and puts forward views and opinions assertively	
96. Looks to improve and upgrade skills and/or knowledge	

Characteristic	Score
97. Is comfortable in a changing environment	
98. Makes timely quality decisions	
99. Holds self accountable for the delivery of results	
100. Encourages debate and open discussion	
101. Values teamwork and working as part of a team	
102. Is attentive to emotional cues and to the unexpressed needs of others	
103. Challenges others' opinions assertively when it is appropriate to do so	
104. Views life long learning as important	
105. Views change as an opportunity to grow and develop	
106. Creates solutions to problems through thorough analysis	
107. Organises own time effectively to deliver the best result	
108. Listens well, seeks mutual understanding and welcomes viewpoints of others	
109. Operates from a place of hope rather than fear of failure	
110. Takes responsibility for reaching solutions, even where others are involved	
111. Proactively takes on challenging roles and tasks	
112. Enjoys learning new things or participating in new activities	

Characteristic	Score
113. Understands the dangers of inertia; always open to the signs of the changing tide	
114. Alters their decisions in the light of new information	
115. Sets high standards of performance for self	
116. Asks open and astute questions to fully understand the issues	
117. Doesn't allow disabling emotions to take control (e.g. fear, anger, anxiety)	
118. Shows sensitivity and understanding to others	
119. Persists despite setbacks	
120. Actively engages in learning events	
121. Questions accepted and traditional approaches; asks "how can it be done better?"	
122. Draws sound inferences from information available	
123. Sets challenging personal targets and strives to exceed them	
124. Initiates actions/events specifically to allow opportunities for relationship-building	
125. Sees the glass as half full rather than half empty	
126. Is able to regulate their emotions to match the needs of the situations, i.e. can regulate their level of empathy in a crisis so that they can take action	
127. Doesn't shirk responsibility	
128. Acts based on own conviction rather than desire to please others	

SCORING

Sixteen dimensions relating to work style effectiveness were measured in this question-naire which are broken down into four main headings as illustrated in Figure 4 below.

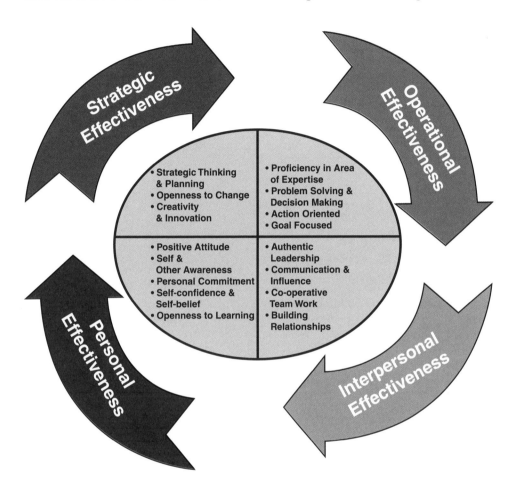

Figure 4: WSEM Model

As shown in the figure, the Work Style Effectiveness Model includes the following subcategories:

Strategic Effectiveness

- Strategic Thinking and Planning
- Openness to Change
- Creativity and Innovation

Operational Effectivenss

- Proficiency in Area of Expertise
- Problem Solving and Decision Making
- Action Oriented
- Goal Focused

Interpersonal Effectiveness

- Authentic Leadership
- Communication and Influence
- Co-operative Teamwork
- Building Relationships

Personal Effectiveness

- Positive Attitude
- Self and Other Awareness
- Personal Commitment
- Self-confidence and Self-belief
- Openness to Learning.

After you have tallied your responses you will interpret your scores on each of the dimensions. To determine your scores:

1. Go to the **Scoring Key** which is on the next page.

2. **Transfer your answers** to the inventory item indicated on the Scoring Key to the space provided.

3. **Add up your answers** to each dimension to obtain your total score for that dimension.

4. **Divide your total score** by the number of items on that dimension to obtain your average score. Note: All dimensions have eight items.

5. **Plot your scores on the WSEM graph**. Place a mark above the dimension being measured at the correct point for each of your scores. Join all your marks together once you have completed this step to produce your profile.

Strategic Effectiveness

Strategic Thinking & Planning	Openness to Change	Creativity & Innovation
1 _____	9 _____	2 _____
14 _____	73 _____	26 _____
25 _____	81 _____	34 _____
33 _____	89 _____	42 _____
41 _____	97 _____	50 _____
49 _____	105 _____	58 _____
57 _____	113 _____	66 _____
65 _____	121 _____	74 _____
Total _____	Total _____	Total _____
Divide by 8	Divide by 8	Divide by 8
Average _____	Average _____	Average _____

Operational Effectiveness

Proficiency in Area of Expertise	Problem Solving & Decision Making	Action Oriented	Goal Focused
4 _____	3 _____	6 _____	5 _____
19 _____	18 _____	21 _____	20 _____
43 _____	82 _____	36 _____	35 _____
51 _____	90 _____	60 _____	91 _____
59 _____	98 _____	68 _____	99 _____
67 _____	106 _____	76 _____	107 _____
75 _____	114 _____	77 _____	115 _____
83 _____	122 _____	84 _____	123 _____
Total _____	Total _____	Total _____	Total _____
Divide by 8	Divide by 8	Divide by 8	Divide by 8
Average _____	Average _____	Average _____	Average _____

Interpersonal Effectiveness

Authentic Leadership	Communication & Influence	Co-operative Teamwork	Building Relationships
7 _____	8 _____	11 _____	10 _____
22 _____	23 _____	27 _____	24 _____
37 _____	38 _____	40 _____	39 _____
52 _____	53 _____	56 _____	54 _____
69 _____	61 _____	63 _____	55 _____
78 _____	100 _____	80 _____	62 _____
85_____	108 _____	93 _____	124 _____
92 _____	116 _____	101 _____	86 _____
Total _____	Total _____	Total _____	Total _____
Divide by 8	Divide by 8	Divide by 8	Divide by 8
Average _____	Average _____	Average _____	Average _____

Personal Effectiveness

Positive Attitude	Self & Other Awareness	Personal Commit-ment	Self-confidence & Self-belief	Openness to Learning
12 _____	13 _____	15 _____	16 _____	17 _____
28 _____	29 _____	30 _____	31 _____	32 _____
44 _____	45 _____	46 _____	47 _____	48 _____
64 _____	70 _____	71 _____	72 _____	79 _____
87 _____	88 _____	94 _____	95 _____	96 _____
109 _____	102 _____	110 _____	103 _____	104 _____
117 _____	118 _____	119 _____	111 _____	112 _____
125 _____	126 _____	127 _____	128 _____	120 _____
Total _____	Total _____	Total _____	Total _____	Total _____
Divide by 8	Divide by 8	Divide by 8	Divide by 8	Divide by 8
Average _____	Average _____	Average _____	Average _____	Average _____

78

Your WSEM Graph

	STP	OC	C&I	PE	PS&M	AO	GF	AL	C&Inf	CTW	BR	PA	PC	S& OA	SC& SB	OL
6.0																
5.0																
4.0																
3.0																
2.0																
1.0																
0.0																

KEY:
STP = Strategic Thinking & Planning; OC = Openness to Change; C&I = Creativity & Innovation; PE = Proficiency in Area of Experise; PS&DM = Problem Solving & Decision Making; AO = Action Oriented; GF = Goal Focused; AL = Authenic Leadership; C&Inf = Communication & Influence; CTW = Co-operative Teamwork; BR = Building Relationships; PA = Positive Attitude; S&OA = Self & Other Awareness; PC = Personal Commitment; SC&SB = Self-confidence & Self-belief; OL = Openness to Learning

INTERPRETATION

Below you will see two descriptions for each of the dimensions assessed in this inventory: a description of a high score and a description of a low score.

These descriptions are idealised – everyone is unique – therefore, the description may not fit you exactly. As you read the description, underline the characteristics which you feel are particularly meaningful to you.

Although a score of "3" or less can be considered a low score, and a score of "4" or above can be considered a high score, the closer to "1" that you score the more the low score describes you, while the closer to "6" that you score, the more the high score describes you. If you scored in the moderate range (2.5 to 4.5), you will probably find that some statements in both descriptions apply to you. Underline those statements.

If you find that all your scores are in the "3" to "4" range, this either means that you are unsure about your effectiveness in this area (perhaps you haven't developed them yet), or that your answers reflect what is known as response bias – a tendency to select answers from the middle of a scale. Go back and examine your answers in order to determine which of these explanations best characterise you.

In interpreting your results, remember that the results of any questionnaire are only a guideline; they are not the definitive picture of your work style effectiveness. If the descriptions below are not consistent with how you see yourself, ask someone who knows you well for their perceptions of your behaviour. Where are the points of similarity and difference?

If you don't like some aspects of your behaviour which are described here and you believe that they are true of you, you can develop a plan to change these behaviours. The sections on Personal Development Activities and the Development Activity Menu will help you in this regard.

Sometimes strengths which are overplayed can become weaknesses and having scores at the extreme of the scale can be problematic. For example, you may have scored a "6" for Action Orientation and a "2" for Collaboration and Co-operation. On the surface you might consider that Action Orientation is a strength but in the light of your low score on Collaboration and Co-operation it could end up being a weakness as people may find you overbearing and pushy. Take a helicopter view of your overall scores and look at the relationship between your scores and the sixteen areas. Common sense is needed when interpreting the results.

STRATEGIC EFFECTIVENESS

Strategic Thinking and Planning

This dimension looks at planning ahead, incorporating short-term goal-setting into long-term plans and the ability to see the connections between related areas.

High Scores

Individuals who score high in this area are more likely to plan ahead when making decisions or analysing situations. They are more likely to anticipate and plan for future events and less likely to be caught off-guard by unforeseen circumstances. When developing plans they work from a broad canvas taking a range of issues or factors into consideration, and they look for the relationships and connections between these different factors. They imagine future possibilities and operate from a "big picture" perspective. If they don't back-up their strategic plans with hard facts and data their plans can turn out to be unrealistic and ultimately fail.

Low Scores

Scores at the low end suggests more short-term immediate approaches to planning. These individuals are more likely to look to the here and now and are less likely to focus on the future. They are less likely to engage in objective analysis and planning. Individuals at this end of the spectrum may prefer action to contemplation. They may be too reactive to the concerns of the moment and may find that they create problems for themselves in the short term by not taking a longer-term view.

Openness to Change

Openness to change is about being responsive to the changing needs in the environment and accepting that change is a fact of life and must be embraced.

High Scores

The change dimension measures the degree to which an individual can deal with and is comfortable with change. Individuals with high scores tend to be more flexible and open to change, seeing change as a constant. They are comfortable with the ambiguity that change brings and do not need to have the complete picture before they act. They are more questioning of traditional approaches and ask "how can it be done better". They may in their eagerness for change find the routine and the mundane difficult and can be easily distracted by the new and the novel.

Low Scores

Individuals with lower scores on the change dimension are more concerned about preserving what is and are not inclined to seek out changes either in the work they do or in their personal lives. They look for security and for preserving the status quo and can come across at times as quite inflexible. They may become stressed in a fast changing environment and become rigid about the smallest of changes as a consequence.

Creativity and Innovation

This is about coming up with creative and innovative approaches to issues and problems. It is about applying creative solutions to making improvements and being comfortable in an environment that encourages creative thinking and innovation.

High Scores

Creativity and innovation are often key to the success of a business, particularly during strategic planning and when designing new products and services. Individuals with high scores in this area like the creative process of "blue sky" thinking and coming up with novel and different ways of doing things. They are more likely to be open to taking risks and trying out new ideas. They also become bored easily with the mundane and the routine and may have a tendency to throw the baby out with the bath water. They may be overly optimistic and not see the downside of the creative ideas presented and the practical barriers to realising them.

Low Scores

Individuals with lower scores in this area look to what they know to come up with solutions rather than thinking outside the box. They may cover the same ground over and over again when trying to generate solutions to problems when what is needed is a completely fresh approach. They are less comfortable with blue sky thinking and generating ideas which appear to have no practical relevance. They like to work with what they know and don't believe in innovating for innovation sake. If they do innovate, they will do so on the basis of what they know and what is already created. There is less of a concern for challenging assumptions and seeking out different ways of doing things. They are more averse to taking risks and may find fast-paced environments uncomfortable. There is a risk of relying too heavily on the current situation and may fail to develop or see new opportunities.

OPERATIONAL EFFECTIVENESS

Proficiency in Area of Expertise

This is about having an in-depth knowledge of one's area of expertise, of being interested in keeping up to date in their own field and continually looking to refine and update their skills and knowledge so that they will be proficient.

High Scores

These individuals have honed and refined their knowledge and skills in their area of expertise. They keep up to-date with what is happening in their area and are seen by others as credible and proficient in applying their skills and knowledge in their chosen field. They ensure their skills and knowledge are relevant for today's market. They are members of their own professional body or society and regularly attend events that keep them abreast of what is happening in their area. They enjoy exercising their skills and knowledge and they bring a great deal of professionalism to their area of expertise.

Low Scores

Individuals who scored low on this dimension have a superficial understanding or application of their area of expertise. They have little interest in honing or perfecting their skills in their chosen field. They rarely read up on what is happening in their area and they have no particular allegiance or affiliation to any professional group or society associated with their chosen field.

Problem Solving and Decision Making

This is about being able to shift through relevant and irrelevant information to effectively solve a problem or to come to a successful decision.

High Scores

Individuals who score high in this area are good at solving complex problems and like the challenges that this poses. They are quick to identify connections and patterns to solutions that others will overlook. They can remain focused on the main problem without getting side-tracked and they provide well thought through solutions and conclusions. They also make timely quality decisions. They may be overly analytical, making a problem or decision more complex than it actually is.

Low Scores

People with scores at the low end will find the task of weighting up the pros and cons of a problem too slow and laborious and will be less critical of information that is presented to them, tending to take it on face value. Their problem solving will be of the simple straightforward kind and their decision making may not be very reliable. Relying too much on their gut instinct could result in missing important information pertinent to the problem, and similarly their lightweight analysis may not instil confidence in others regarding their decisions.

Action Oriented

This area is about making things happen and seizing opportunities when they arise and acting on them. It is about looking for immediate results and staying close to the action.

High Scores

Higher scores on the action orientation dimension are characteristic of individuals who make things happen. They have multiple projects and/or tasks on the go and bring a lot of energy and enthusiasm to the ones they are involved in. They like to be in the centre of the action and drive things along with their engagement. Because they are so enthusiastic they inspire others to action. They are highly opportunistic, always on the look out for potential opportunities. Because they are always on the go and like to be busy they find it hard to stand back and reflect, which means they may miss important information that might help them more easily succeed.

Low Scores

Individuals who score low on this dimension may miss golden opportunities because they are too slow in making things happen. They may have a tendency to be too reflective about ideas and plans and take too long in getting a result. Their perfectionist standards and their unwillingness to move things along at a faster pace can allow others to steal a march on their ideas. They are not as opportunistic as they should be and may allow great opportunities and ideas to pass them by. They will bring great dedication to one or two areas and will be seen as reliable and persistent.

Goal Focused

This is about setting clear goals and targets and holding oneself and others accountable for delivering on them. The focus is on results and measuring the attainment of outcomes.

High Scores

Individuals with higher scores are perceived as holding high expectations for themselves. They will often be seen as pushing themselves to achieve even greater successes and overcome greater challenges. They are very goal-oriented and set clear and challenging goals which they track and monitor on a regular basis. They are interested in results and they create a challenging results-oriented environment. Those who score high may hold unreasonable expectations and end up bruising their own and others' morale. They may also be too demanding and unsympathetic of self and others.

Low Scores

Individuals who score low put less pressure on themselves; they go with the flow and have no clear sense of direction or purpose. They rarely set clear goals and targets and when they do they have a tendency to ignore them, thus not achieving the results they set out to accomplish. They may not think of end outcomes or results but expect that things will automatically happen. They may set the bar too low for themselves and never really achieve their full potential.

INTERPERSONAL EFFECTIVENESS

Authentic Leadership

Authentic Leadership is about being in tune with your own passions and beliefs, stepping out and acting on these insights and inspiring others to respond through your actions.

High Scores

Higher scores on this dimension are characteristic of those who feel passionate about an issue or situation and as a result engage and inspire others to act. They are not afraid to stand up and take a stand and can get things done through others. They are in tune with their beliefs and values, and their leadership is about serving the greater good and not just about personal ambition. They will not shy away from taking up a leadership role when necessary, regardless of status or standing, because they feel motivated to act. They generate pride, commitment and trust in others.

Low Scores

Individuals with lower scores are less likely to step out and act on what they feel strongly about. They are uncomfortable taking a stand even when they feel passionate about an issue and believe action is required. They don't tend to push themselves forward into the public arena, preferring to keep a low profile. They are more comfortable being a follower than a leader, never fully realising their own true voice. They may not be as in tune with their values and beliefs because they don't take the time to explore them.

Communication and Influence

This area is about using communication and influence to change others' thinking. It employs the skills of listening, encouraging open discussion and debate and using different influencing tactics.

High Scores

Higher scores indicate someone who is comfortable influencing and negotiating with others. Their communication is clear and succinct and has a way of engaging others in the discussion and debate. They are able to influence people's thinking and change their point of view and are very comfortable in this area. They use the full range of the communication spectrum to best effect. They may appear overly pushy to some people particularly, when they feel strongly about an issue.

Low Scores

Individuals with low scores are more comfortable going with the consensus than pushing their own point of view onto others. They are less likely to try to influence others around to their perspective and will go with the group consensus. They tend not to hold strong views on issues and will be seen by others as amenable and easy going, if at times a little wishy washy because they rarely take a strong stance. They may be subject to the whims of others if they don't learn to speak up and take a stand.

Co-operative Teamwork

This area is about valuing the importance of working as part of a team. It's about sharing information with others and helping the team achieve its goals over and above their own interests and goals.

High Scores

Individuals with high scores actively participate and engage in team projects. They genuinely believe that more can be accomplished through team effort and they willingly muck in and do their share of the work. They value the input and expertise of others and encourage them to participate as part of the team. They are less likely to pursue their own status or gain at the expense of other team members. They may hide behind the team, never taking responsibility for their own decisions.

Low Scores

Individuals with lower scores prefer an individualist rather than a team approach. They are focused more on their own priorities and less concerned with being helpful to others. They are happier working on their own or don't see the value of pooling resources and tapping into the expertise of others. Recognition and status are important to them so they will favour activities where they can personally be honoured. They may be seen as selfish by others and egotistical in their need for recognition.

Building Relationships

This is about developing and building positive relationships with others and about being at ease in social situations.

High Scores

Individuals who score high in this area are often friendly and outgoing, and possess good interpersonal skills. They are relaxed in most social settings, able to strike up a conversation easily with strangers. People generally find them warm and approachable and are willing to open up and confide in them. They generally have a wide range of networks which they draw on when needed. They initiate actions or events specifically to allow opportunities for relationship building. Because they are quite the social butterfly some people may find them overbearing or shallow.

Low Scores

Individuals with scores on the low end are less comfortable in social situations and may find meeting new people and striking up a conversation difficult. Their interactions with others are more task-based and they rarely engage in social niceties in order to build better relationships. Individuals who score on the low end are happiest in a job in which they can exercise some control over how much time they spend with other people. They can appear shy with people they don't know very well, and are uncomfortable in situations in which they are expected to socialise. Because they often avoid or feel uncomfortable in social situations, some people may perceive them as aloof or standoffish.

PERSONAL EFFECTIVENESS

Positive Attitude

This area is about having a positive and optimistic approach to life and being able to maintain focus and remain optimistic even under difficult circumstances.

High Scores

Individuals with high scores tend to be enthusiastic and believe in a positive outcome. They operate from a place of hope rather than fear. They are able to maintain their motivation and deal with frustrations when things don't go according to plan, channelling their energy into something more positive. They are also capable of generating a range of coping mechanisms to deal with both mundane and difficult situations. They manage their emotions in stressful situations and are not prone to outbursts. They may be overly optimistic and irritate others with their Pollyanna-type attitude.

Low Scores

Individuals who score low in this area tend to be more critical by nature and see the negative side of a situation. They can be quick to spot flaws in a situation or an individual. They can be good problem solvers or trouble shooters but may over-emphasise this quality in other areas of their life unnecessarily. They hail from the "glass is half empty" brigade and their negativity can have a draining effect on others. They will typically be more cautious by nature, less likely to take a risk without careful analysis and evaluation.

Self and Other Awareness

This area is about having a well developed sense of oneself and others. It is about being able to accurately read emotions, both one's own and those of others, and to use them to best effect.

High Scores

Scores at the high end indicate someone who can accurately interpret their own and others' feelings and put them to good use. They demonstrate a sophisticated awareness of the impact of their own behaviour on others. They are able to read relationships well, picking up subtle positive and negative cues. They are also able to read between the lines and note what people aren't saying, picking up the emotional messages others are giving off. They can manage their emotions to match the needs of the situation, that is, they can regulate their level of empathy in a crisis so that they can take appropriate action. Because of their sensitivity to others they may be seen as too soft or overly sensitive.

Low Scores

Individuals with lower scores are not comfortable with emotions, theirs or others'. They see little reason for the need to respond to the emotional needs of others. They may choose to keep a certain distance from other people. Because they are so out of tune with their emotions other people may experience their emotional responses or reactions as disproportionate relative to the situation. They are also more likely to be prone to inappropriate outbursts. They will be less likely to pick up on the non-verbal content of a discourse between individuals and may be seen as cool and aloof, as well as being clumsy in handling more sensitive issues.

Personal Commitment

This area is about taking the initiative and not shirking responsibility. It is about seeing projects through and being able to stay focused on the task at hand, typically being able to delay gratification.

High Scores

Individuals with higher scores try to overcome obstacles and don't give up easily. They make suggestions or bring new ideas without them being solicited. They take responsibility for reaching solutions, even where others are involved, and they don't dump responsibility onto others' shoulders. They anticipate situations and act to create opportunities that are not obvious to others. Very high scorers may be likely to rush in and fix the problem even when it might be wiser or more appropriate not to do so.

Low Scores

Individuals who score low tend to look for the easy way out. They are not as driven to find a resolution or to take responsibility. They are more comfortable being told what to do and receiving instruction from someone in authority. They will be less likely to jump in to deal with a situation, instead standing back and waiting to see how it unfolds. They value play over work and can allow it to get in the way of a satisfactory outcome. They may be reluctant to take the initiative and hence they and others may lose out on their insightful ideas.

Self-confidence and Self-belief

This area is about being confident in one's beliefs and asserting one's views and opinions when appropriate. It is about having the confidence in one's ability to succeed.

High Scores

Individuals with higher scores are perceived as being willing to stand up for what they believe even if it proves unpopular. They present themselves with a self-assured confidence and have presence. They can voice views and options that are unpopular and often go out on a limb for what they believe in. They are also assertive with others and willing to challenge their viewpoints. They act based on their own conviction rather than a desire to please others. Because of their strong self-belief they may come across as overly arrogant.

Low Scores

Individuals who score low tend to hold back from pushing themselves forward. They may have the appearance of being vulnerable and sensitive and appreciate it when more dominant individuals take them under their wing. Though they may have strong views and opinions they may not always get a hearing and as a result others can miss out on their insights.

Openness to Learning

Openness to Learning is about the willingness to invest in one's own development and believing that life long learning is essential. It is also about being open to feedback in order to enhance effectiveness and looking to upgrade and develop skills.

High Scores

Individuals who score high in this area make a concerted effort to upgrade and develop their skills on a regular basis. They are willing to invest in their own development and are comfortable seeking feedback on their performance in order to enhance their effectiveness. They are aware of their strengths and their weaknesses and know how to get the best from themselves. They are open to different perspectives and ways of doing things and keep up to date in their own area of interest, as well as having a keen interest in learning new things or trying out new activities that are outside their normal sphere of activity. Those on the higher end may make a profession out of learning and never get around to practically applying it.

Low Scores

Individuals with lower scores tend to rely on what they learnt in school or college/university as a means to achieving success. They are more inclined to fine-tune and develop what they already know than look to develop new skills. They are not as open to learning as they should be and close themselves off from opportunities to engage in learning events. They rarely solicit feedback on their performance and may find that their skills and knowledge have become dated. They are sceptical of other professions or technical specialisms which are not related to their area of interest or activity.

DEVELOPING YOUR WSEM PROFILE

In order to put together your WSEM profile you will need to develop your "Personal Profile" which highlights your strengths and development areas and your "Job Profile" which outlines what is important for the role you hold and/or aspire to. Below is an outline of how you will go about doing that, coupled with a profile table for each area.

Step One: Compiling Your "Personal Profile"

Go back to your scoring key. What are your highest and lowest scores? You may only have two "extreme" scores, or you may have several. You should categorise your scores accordingly:

- Higher scores = clear strengths – you are a role model in this area
- Moderate scores = not quite fully a strength – there are some development areas
- Lower scores = clearly a development area.

List up to two or three in each of the high, moderate and low categories.

Sample Personal Profile Table

	High	Medium	Low
Creativity and Innovation	✓		
Co-operative Teamwork			✓
Communication & Influence	✓		
Authentic Leadership		✓	
Self-confidence & Self-belief			✓
Strategic Thinking			✓
Proficiency in Area of Expertise	✓		
Action Oriented		✓	
Positive Attitude		✓	
Etc.			

Your Personal Profile Table

	High	Medium	Low

Step Two: Compiling Your "Job Profile"

In mapping out your development goals you will need to think about the requirements of your current role and any future roles you aspire to. To help you do this consider one or all of the following:

* In your current role or a role you have applied for, what types of activities are involved? How might the role evolve over time in light of the economic and organisational changes which might occur?

* Your work-related objectives and measurable targets over the next 12 months

* Your future aspirations regarding your role and your career.

Using the above areas as a guide, ask yourself the following questions and note your answers in the table provided below. A sample "job profile" has been completed.

1. What are the overall objectives for your current role and any role you have applied for?

2. What skill, knowledge, and behaviours would you expect of someone successfully fulfilling that role now and in the future?

3. Given the aspirations you may have for your role and your career, what skills will you need, what behaviours will be important to demonstrate and what knowledge will you require?

When you have noted down the skills, knowledge and behaviours for the above, decide which of the 16 WSEM areas are most important for your current role and your future aspirations. The 16 WSEM areas are not exhaustive so you may find that there isn't a neat fit; if not, put in your own WSEM Area which you feel captures what is required. You might find that one objective covers two or three WSEM areas. If that is the case, either decide which is the most important or put down all that apply.

Sample:

Objective for Role: To design and deliver training modules in specialist subjects

Future Aspiration: To set up and run a training company

Current Role Requirements	Skills, Knowledge, Behaviours	WSEM Area
To come up with creative ideas and novel concepts to enhance an individual's learning	Brainstorm ideas, generate creative ways of presenting material; develop models	Creativity & Innovation
To be able to present to large groups in a confident manner	Poise, calmness, comfortable with groups	Self-confidence & Self-belief
To have in-depth knowledge in specialist areas	Knowledge of accounts and accounting software packages	Proficiency in Area of Expertise
Future Role Requirements	**Skills, Knowledge, Behaviours**	**WSEM Area**
To develop a network of business contacts	Develop relationships; look for synergies between what I am offering and what they need	Building Relationships

Current Role Requirements	Skills, Knowledge, Behaviours	WSEM Area
To write and present business proposals	Write proposals in a way that appeals to the needs of the audience	Communication & Influence
To think long term about how the business should be positioned and who the key audience should be	Knowledge of the current environment, ability to plan, and link plans to business needs of clients	Strategic Thinking & Planning

"Job Profile" Table

Objective for Role: _____

Future Aspiration: _____

Current Role Requirements	Skills, Knowledge, Behaviours	WSEM Area

Future Role Requirements	Skills, Knowledge, Behaviours	WSEM Area

Step Three: Compiling Your "WSEM Profile"

The next stage in the personal development process is to bring these two profiles together so that you can clearly see how your strengths match the requirements of your current and future roles, and from there produce a list of the areas you need to acquire or enhance, i.e. your development needs.

Transfer the WSEM areas which you identified as important for your role now and into the future to the table below by ticking or highlighting the relevant boxes. Now transfer the list from your Personal Profile to the table below, again by ticking the appropriate boxes for your strengths and your development needs.

You should now be able to work out those areas which you need to develop by looking at the table and matching the areas relevant to your job and future aspirations with your development needs. Where a WSEM area and a personal profile area are at odds, tick the personal development need box.

Sample WSEM Profile Table

	Job Relevant Areas	Strength	Development Need	Personal Development Need
Strategic Effectiveness				
Strategic Thinking & Planning	✓		✓	✓
Openness to Change	✓			
Creativity & Innovation		✓		
Operational Effectiveness				
Proficiency in Area of Expertise	✓	✓		
Problem Solving & Decision Making				
Action Oriented			✓	
Goal Focused				

	Job Relevant Areas	Strength	Development Need	Personal Development Need
Interpersonal Effectiveness				
Authentic Leadership			✓	
Communication & Influence	✓		✓	✓
Building Relationships	✓			
Teamwork		✓		
Personal Effectiveness				
Positive Attitude			✓	
Self & Other Awareness				
Personal Commitment				
Self-confidence & Self-belief	✓		✓	✓
Openness to Learning				

Interpretation of "WSEM Profile" Table

The strengths the individual brings to their current role are Creativity & Innovation and Proficiency in Area of Expertise and for their future role, Communication & Influence.

Areas for development based on current role are Self-confidence and Self-belief and for the future role it is Strategic Thinking and Planning. These areas become the priority to focus on over the next 12 months. You will notice that Authentic Leadership is also a development need but not considered important to the role. Given the future aspirations of the individual they may want to add Authentic Leadership to their development plans.

One area that is not captured in their personal profile is Building Relationships yet it is considered to be important to their future aspirations. They will need to revisit the WSEM graph and see whether this is a strength or a development need and add it to their WSEM profile.

Assessing Your Work Style Effectiveness

Now complete your own WSEM Profile. Once this is done you are ready to move on to the next two chapters. Chapter Seven is Reality Testing and Soliciting Feedback. This chapter will give you an opportunity to validate your own insights by soliciting feedback from others. Getting good quality feedback from other people will enhance what you have begun in this chapter, and once you have a clear picture of your development needs you are ready to start putting together a development plan.

Chapter Eight will give you some invaluable tips and hints as to what you might do to strengthen your talents (areas identified as strengths) and address any weaknesses. As already stated, all sixteen areas are important so once you have mastered your initial development goals you will then want to go on and put together a plan to develop any remaining areas which are not already strengths.

	Job Relevant Areas	Strength	Development Need	Personal Development Need
Strategic Effectiveness				
Strategic Thinking and Planning				
Openness to Change				
Creativity & Innovation				
Operational Effectiveness				
Proficiency in Area of Expertise				
Problem Solving & Decision Making				
Action Oriented				
Goal Focused				
Interpersonal Effectiveness				
Authentic Leadership				
Communication & Influence				
Co-operative Teamwork				
Building Relationships				

	Job Relevant Areas	Strength	Devel- opment Need	Personal Develop- ment Need
Personal Effectiveness				
Positive Attitude				
Self & Other Awareness				
Personal Commitment				
Self-confidence & Self-belief				
Openness to Learning				

WSEM Assessment Summary

In looking at your skills, knowledge and attributes using the WSEM assessment:

1. The areas important for your role are:

_____

_____

_____

_____

_____

_____

_____

2. Your talents or strengths are:

_____

_____

_____

_____

_____

_____

_____

3. Your personal development needs are:

_____

_____

_____

_____

_____

_____

_____

4. The development actions you might take are:

_____

_____

_____

_____

_____

_____

7

Reality Testing – Soliciting Feedback from Others

"Oh would some power the gift he give us,
To see ourselves as others see us." – Robert Burns

You have now completed a detailed analysis of your strengths and development needs using the WSEM. From Section Two you also have a very clear picture of your style, interests, values and work preferences; you may also have begun to formulate some tentative career goals and/or some ways of enriching your present position.

The next step is to move beyond self-analysis to gather information about how other people see you. No matter how honest and thoughtful we are in assessing ourselves, we all have certain blind spots. Others may point to weaknesses we are unaware of or, more commonly, strengths and abilities we have underestimated. Moreover, even when others' views generally confirm your own, that input will still help clarify and round out your picture of yourself.

Obviously no two people will see you in exactly the same way. Neither is it true that other people will always see you more accurately than you see yourself. By talking to a range of people whose opinion you value, you will develop an enhanced picture of how the world sees you. This section tells you how to go about the process of testing out the results of your self-analysis.

WHOSE FEEDBACK DO YOU VALUE?

Write down the names of people whose opinion you value and who have had the opportunity to observe you. Consider, for example, your:

- Current and past managers
- Peers/colleagues

100

- Direct reports or employees
- Friends and family members
- Mentors/coaches/guides
- Teachers, lectures, tutors.

Use the following guidelines to help you. The person:
- Has observed your performance in different situations
- Knows you well and how you tend to react to different situations
- Is supportive of your own best interests
- Is perceptive – you value their opinion.

People whose opinion I value:

_____

_____

_____

_____

WHAT IS THE NATURE OF THE FEEDBACK YOU WANT FROM EACH OF THEM?

The nature and kind of feedback you solicit from each of the people you have identified will, of course, depend on the nature of your relationship with them.

Your manager and other work contacts are obviously an important source of information about your performance-related behaviour and potential. There are two approaches you can take in order to solicit feedback:

Approach 1: You may want to engage in general discussion with others about your strengths and development areas, career path and potential based on your own self-analysis using the tools contained within this workbook.

Approach 2: You may want others to complete a questionnaire (typically known as a 360° questionnaire) based on the requirements of your role. There are a number of such questionnaires on the market. This will give you a fuller picture of your strengths and development areas. Feedback should ideally be obtained from a more senior person to you, for example, your manger, or a mentor; peers, if you are a manage, the people who report to you; and from customers if appropriate. Alternatively, you can ask people to complete the WSEM on you and you can compare others' views against your own.

Approach 1: General Discussion – Feedback

Below are a list of questions you may want to ask your manager and other significant work contacts, colleagues or friends:

* What do you see are my major skills and strengths?
* What do you see are my major development areas?
* How can I improve how I am seen by others?
* What are the main areas I should be working on improving over the next year?
* Given what you know of me at the present time:
    ◊ What kind of jobs (levels, etc.) do you think I could realistically aspire to over the next few years?
    ◊ Are you aware of any jobs that I would perform well in?
    ◊ How realistic do you think my career goals are based on what I've told you?
    ◊ What kind of training and/or development do you feel I need to attain these goals?
    ◊ In terms of attaining these goals, is there anything you think I (should pay particular attention to?) (watch out for?) (work on improving?)
    ◊ Do you see any obstacles to my accomplishing my goals?
    ◊ Are my interests (plans, goals, etc.) consistent with what you know about my personality and ability?
* What kind of developmental experiences would help me accomplish my goals?

Approach 2: 360° Questionnaire – Feedback

One way for us to get a better insight into ourselves and the impact that we have on others is through 360° degree feedback. This is a process in which you as a individual receive both quantitative and qualitative feedback on your performance against a set of criteria important to a given job. The name refers to the 360 degrees of a circle and to the fact that the individuals invited to provide feedback to you represent the full circle of people with whom you regularly work. In addition to rating oneself, the feedback circle can include direct reports, peers, internal or external customers, your boss, partner or friends.

360° feedback offers many potential benefits. Because the technique utilises multiple perspectives, the results are considered highly credible and provide useful performance feedback. A 360° experience can help to confirm hunches about strengths and identify areas that need improvement. Being able to compare feedback from multiple sources helps you contrast your self-perceptions with others' perceptions of you. But the benefits of this kind of reality check also have their challenges. Receiving feedback of this kind can be surprising, powerful and uncomfortable. It is important that as much emphasis is paid to one's strengths as to one's development needs. To make sense of the data, you should link the results of your 360° to previous performance feedback, look for performance themes and issues and understand how to use the results to be more successful. Positive change is the ultimate goal of any 360° feedback.

WHO SHOULD YOU GIVE THE QUESTIONNAIRE TO?

It is up to you to identify who you'd like to get feedback from if you are currently employed. You certainly should include your current or previous boss, and it is recommended that you include the following, if appropriate:

- Up to three colleagues, i.e. those people on the same level as you (minimum two)
- Up to three people who report to you (minimum two)
- Clients or customers (minimum two)
- Past co-workers or supervisors, friends, mentors or coaches.

The best people to choose are those who know you well and who you often work with. It is important that they can remember a number of experiences where they either worked with you, or observed you at work. They should be people who, from a range of perspectives, will be able to give you honest, positive and constructive feedback on how they see you.

What Tools Are Available?

You can use the WSEM questionnaire as a good starting place. You can use the long version by getting your chosen group of people to assess you on each of the questions on the questionnaire and then score them as you did for yourself, plotting each response on the graph. Or you can use the shortened version of the WSEM using the 16 dimensions and again getting your chosen group of people to assess you on their perceptions of your effectiveness using a scale of 1 to 6 (one being low and six being high) on each dimension.

What Do You Need to Do?

- Decide which questionnaire or approach you wish to use.
- Speak to each person you have selected to ensure they understand why you are requesting their feedback and to encourage them to participate. Find out what

the deadline for completion of questionnaires is and make sure you and the other respondents stick to it.

- Forward the questionnaire to each individual providing details on what is involved, why you are seeking their feedback and how the results will be used.

- Book an appointment to talk to your employer or coach on foot of the feedback, about what you have learnt, and what you want to start, continue or stop doing.

Guidelines for Feedback Discussions

- Plan your questions ahead of time. Know what you want to share of your self-assessment data. Know what you want to achieve in each meeting.

- Create a climate in which the other person will feel comfortable sharing their perceptions of you.

- Listen. Don't be defensive. Don't punish the other person for being wrong. Ask for examples of specific behaviours, both positive and negative. Discuss and probe until you clearly understand the feedback. For example, if your boss says, "You don't meet your deadlines", you can respond, "Could you be more specific? Could you give me an example?"

- Ask for guidelines and examples on what you can do to improve your weaknesses and change your behaviour, e.g. "What do you think I should be doing differently?"

- Make notes during the discussion.

- Don't immediately reject out-of-hand feedback you receive. Even if it doesn't seem accurate to you, go away and consider it. If you don't hear the same feedback from anyone else, then you may want to consider rejecting it as not very significant.

- Express appreciation for the other person's time and honesty.

- You may want to send a thank you note to someone who has been particularly helpful.

- Remember that no one is perfect. So you have some weaknesses – welcome to the club!

Summary of Feedback Discussions

Note down below the main areas for development based on your discussions and/ or feedback from the 360 questionnaire.

Development Options

1. What are the main themes or messages that are coming through for you about your strengths and development needs?

_____

_____

_____

_____

_____

_____

2. What key areas do you specifically need to focus on? What ideas or suggestions were made as to how you might go about this?

_____

_____

_____

_____

_____

_____

3. In what broad areas would you like to make improvements?

_____

_____

_____

_____

_____

_____

4. What first steps might you take?

_____

_____

_____

_____

_____

_____

8

Development Options

*"I do the best I know how, the very best I can; and I mean to keep
on doing it to the end."* – Abraham Lincoln

At this stage you should have a complete picture of how you see yourself and how others see you. You should also have a good sense of your talents and what it is you need to develop.

Development is an ongoing process. Once you have mastered one set of behaviours, or acquired a new set of skills or knowledge, it pushes the door open further to more learning and development opportunities.

The Boyatzis model of self-directed learning, outlined below, nicely encapsulates the learning cycle that you have been experiencing in this workbook. According to Boyatzis, to successfully grow and develop individuals must go through five core stages, which Daniel Goleman termed "discoveries" in his book *The New Leaders: Transforming the Art of Leadership into the Science of Results.*

The first discovery is getting a clear picture of your ideal self – who it is you want to be. Part Two of this workbook was all about making that discovery. Having a clear picture of your ideal self or career is the motivating force which keeps you on track. We will expand on this theme in Part Four when we look at your vision for your life; this will further enhance your understanding of who you are and what you want to be.

The second discovery is having an understanding of your real self – your strengths and your weaknesses. The WSEM model, and the feedback you received from others, should have given you a comprehensive pictures of your strengths and development needs.

The third discovery is about developing your learning plan based on the discrepancy between your ideal self and your real self. This section of the workbook is about helping you do just that. It gives you a guide to the development options open to you with some useful suggestions as to how you might go about developing new skills or behaviours against the WSEM model.

The fourth discovery is about practising these new behaviours, or thoughts, until they automatically become part and parcel of who you are. If you are to make fundamental shifts in your learning and development, you will need to go beyond intellectualising them to actually getting out and practicing them until they become a habit (see Kolb's model of experiential learning below.) So once you have drawn up your development plan it is critical that you get out there and do something about it.

The fifth discovery can occur at any time in the process. This is about having a guide, a mentor or a cheerleader to help you work through the different discoveries and to support you in your learning. It is only through your interaction with others that you can truly learn and grow. So if you haven't done so already, now is a good time to enlist the support of a trusted other to help you on your journey of discovery, someone whom you can begin to share what you have learnt about yourself from this workbook.

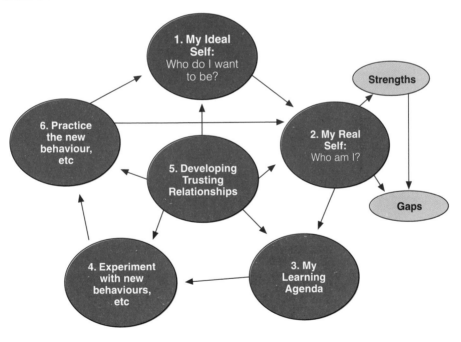

Figure 5: Boyatzis's Theory of Self-Directed Learning

When learning a new behaviour or attitude, or acquiring a new skill or a piece of knowledge (for ease of reference we will refer to this as "your learning agenda"), you typically go through four stages, according to Kolb's theory of learning from his book *Experiential Learning*. Kolb contends that to truly embed and master the learning you should ideally span all four areas below:

- Concrete Experience (Do) is about trying out your "learning agenda".

- Reflective Observation (Reflect) is about reflecting on how well you have done. What worked? What didn't work? How did you feel/think? How did you or others respond?

- Abstract Conceptualisation (Think) is about fitting those reflections back into your model of learning and thinking about how much have you learnt, where you might need to make adjustments and what further help you might need.

- Active Experimentation (Plan) is about planning how you are going to address any shortfalls or gaps and what you will need to do differently to attain mastery of your "learning agenda".

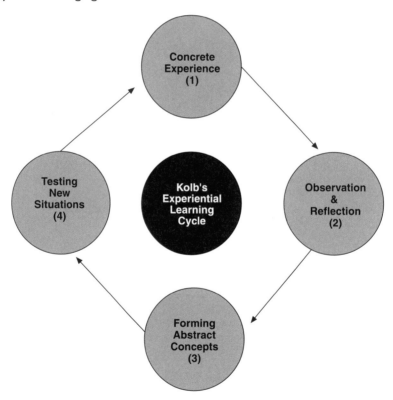

Figure 6: Kolb's Experiential Learning Cycle

Development Options

Kolb's model of experiential learning falls neatly into four learning styles. The styles highlight the conditions under which learners best learn. These styles were further developed by Honey and Mumford and if you are interested in assessing your own preferred learning style you can take their questionnaire on-line at www. peterhoney.com. Knowing your learning style can accelerate your learning by creating the conditions under which you learn best, and it can also help you in avoiding the trap of repeating the same mistake by strengthening other styles of learning. For example, if you always stand back and reflect you can strengthen your learning by getting out and experimenting. Kolb's four styles, explained with Honey and Mumford's titles in brackets, are:

- Accommodating (Activist) is about "having an experience". Individuals with this learning preference get out there and have a go; they do first rather than reflect, are open-minded and enthusiastic, immerse themselves fully in new experiences.

- Diverging (Reflector) is about "reflecting on the experience". Individuals with this learning preference like to stand back and gather data about experiences, delay reaching conclusions, listen before speaking, are thoughtful.

- Assimilating (Theorist) is about "concluding from the experience". Individuals with this learning preference think through problems in a logical manner, are objective, assimilate disparate facts into models and theories, reject subjectivity, look for order.

- Converging (Pragmatist) is about "planning the next steps". Individuals with this learning preference are practical, keen to put ideas into practice, seek out new opportunities to experiment, act quickly, get bored with endless discussion.

So, when planning your development it is worth bearing the following points in mind:

- Your strengths today may become your weaknesses in a future role (being comfortable working on your own for prolonged periods is a strength when you are programming or writing a book, but can become a weakness when you are required to meet clients and generate new business.

- Flaws may suddenly matter; your creative energy and ideas may need to become more realistic and practical.

- Overplayed strengths can become weaknesses – being decisive if overplayed can turn into arrogance.

- Current strengths may be less important in the future – as you progress in your career your technical know-how may take a back seat to important managerial skills.

In this chapter you will find tools that will help you to:

- Learn more about the range of activities that can contribute to personal development
- Become aware of a list of development activities for six of the WSEM areas with a comprehensive list of resources for all sixteen areas at the end of this workbook.

PERSONAL DEVELOPMENT ACTIVITIES

Types of Development Activities

This section provides background information on commonly used development methods that can be applied to any area needing development.

There are many types of activity that can be used to help you develop your skills at work. Think of all the ways in which development can take place. Draw on the activities that you have used for learning in the past and consider new activities that you would like to try out. Add to the list below.

Some Learning Options

Strategic (longer term, more holistic)

- Learning contracts
- Mentors
- Learning groups/sets
- Networking
- Learning organisation
- Organisational development.

Tactical (e.g. particular learning designs)

- Courses
- Workshops
- Seminars
- Conferences
- Projects
- Coaching
- 360° feedback
- Away days

Development Options

- Secondments/job swaps
- Research
- Counselling
- Voluntary work
- Team development
- Development centres
- Distance learning
- Deputising
- Learning resource centres.

Methods/Techniques

- Visits
- Shadowing
- Reading
- CDs
- CD-ROMs
- Interactive DVDs
- Packages
- Internet
- Computer conferencing
- Dialogue
- Presentations
- Writing
- Meditation
- Thinking
- Case studies
- Rewards for learning
- Feedback
- Observation
- Role plays
- Psychometrics
- Simulations.

In this section, we will describe some of the various types of activities so that you can choose the ones most relevant to you. We will concentrate on:

- Open learning
- Books
- Videos/DVDs
- CD-ROMs
- Work-related development activities
- Shadowing
- Mentoring
- Learning networks
- Training courses.

Open Learning

Open learning is an umbrella term that refers to a wide range of ways of learning. It aims to make it as easy as possible for people to acquire and update their skills by using a variety of methods at a time, place and pace to suit their circumstances.

With open learning you can choose:

- What and when to study
- How slow (or fast) to study
- Where to study
- How to study (e.g. you can find your own route through the material, and choose the most appropriate medium)
- How help is provided (e.g. face-to-face, by post, by phone, by computer, in work-groups etc.)
- Who can help (e.g. colleagues, work-based supervisor, tutor, trainer, mentor, friends).

Open learning is attractive to people for its flexibility. This flexibility is achieved by making the optimum use of different media (workbooks, CDs, video/DVDs, film, computer-assisted learning, interactive video).

Books

Just as every journalist is reputed to have a novel in their top drawer, every "expert" and consultant seems to produce a "how to" book. Bearing in mind that no one ever became successful just by reading about it, books can be an extremely useful source of ideas, inspiration and knowledge. They have a part to play in a personal development plan as long as there are opportunities to put into practice the concepts and suggestions contained in them.

DVDs/Videos

DVDs/videos can be useful in conveying key points in an informative, easy to absorb and often entertaining manner. However, they need to be combined with other methods if they are to be fully effective. There is a danger that viewers respond to them as they would to an ordinary TV programme, i.e. watch them and forget them. For this reason they are best used as part of a formal training course, or less formally with groups of viewers where the issues and key points can be discussed and new behaviours practised. Many DVDs/videos now come with trainers' packs including handouts, exercises and overhead slides, which can be used to maximise the benefits.

CD-ROMs

CD-ROMs can be useful in situations when it is difficult to get people together for training exercises or when, for example, it is more convenient for individuals to study when it suits them. One major advantage of CD-ROM training materials is that they are, by nature, interactive; consequently, users don't get the chance to let their attention waver. Most combine graphics, animation and video clips, and each course can be an entertaining and memorable learning experience.

Work-related Development Activities

There are development opportunities which may arise during everyday work. By being involved in small discrete projects, you will have the chance to practice new skills, often in a fairly "safe" environment. Activities which fall outside the range of normal everyday tasks are usually called assignments. Projects and assignments can be particularly useful:

* For stretching you when you need a new challenge
* To prepare you for job changes (by giving you a taste of the new job)
* To broaden the understanding of the business as a whole
* To provide specific experience in a particular area or with a particular issue.

There are two essential things to remember before you embark on a project or assignment:

1. If any particular new skills are needed to complete the assignment, these should be gained first, e.g. a project manager should attend some form of project management training or facilitation skills training

2. Support (from colleagues or managers) should be available.

Shadowing

Shadowing is another good way to get a good appreciation of a different function or different role. It involves spending time with someone (in or outside of the company) who has a different role or way of doing things than you. You can sit in on meetings and assist them wherever possible.

Mentoring

Many successful people report that they have had a "mentor", usually early in their career. A mentor is a senior person who takes a personal interest in your career, who provides opportunities to learn and talk about development. Mentoring can happen informally or formally. The practice of managers formally sponsoring a junior colleague for development purposes can be highly effective if properly planned and monitored. Mentoring that happens on an informal basis can also be effective.

Characteristics of Successful Mentors

*   They draw out the strengths and weaknesses of their people rather than suppressing them

*   They positively seek to identify learning opportunities, e.g. reviewing and analysing an activity for learning purposes

*   They involve their people in some of their own important tasks (i.e. not just delegating the simple or routine tasks)

*   They share some of their problems and anxieties with their people in the interests of their development – not just as relief for themselves

*   They listen rather than talk

*   They do not say or imply "be more like me".

Learning Review Groups

What Are They?

In many cases you can obtain benefits and support from sharing ideas, problems and opportunities with colleagues who are at a similar stage of development. Setting up self-help development groups is one way of enabling people to learn from each other's experiences. They can also provide a forum for participants to try out some of the work-related activities referred to in this section of the handbook.

How Should They Be Used?

Learning networks could take the form of:

- Groups formed to carry out a specific project
- Coaching/learning groups where individuals offer coaching to others in areas in which they have special expertise or experience in return for coaching from others for their own development needs
- Regular workshops to receive feedback on specific areas of competence
- Opportunities to meet and discuss with managers, experts or specialists.

You may want to enlist the help of a training manager to help the network to form, to advise on process issues, to act as a technical expert on training and development issues or to mediate between the network and others for the provision of resources and facilities. Once set up, the routine management of the network should be the responsibility of you yourself. Indeed, running the network is in itself a significant development opportunity.

Training Courses

Formal, off-the-job training courses are still the most common of development activities. There is an enormous variety of courses available, ranging from half-day lectures to five-year Open University degree courses.

When choosing courses, you should consider the following questions:

- Have you set yourself SMART objectives?
- Have you considered alternative methods of development (e.g. on the job)?
- Have you discussed the range of courses available with someone who is knowledgeable in the area of training and development?
- Have you reviewed the detailed course objectives and methods (not just the title) and how you can apply the knowledge to your own job situation?
- Do you know of other people who have been on this course? What were their opinions of it? Have they benefited?
- Do you need to make readjustments in your personal and work life if you undertake a specific course?
- Could this be used as a development opportunity for a colleague or others?
- How will you evaluate any changes in your performance as a result of the course?

THE DEVELOPMENT ACTIVITY MENU

Introduction

This section looks at a range of activities which you can undertake to enhance your work effectiveness in specific areas. For example, if your WSEM Profile indicated that your personal development needs should focus on the areas of Creativity and Innovation, Action Oriented, Authentic Leadership, Positive Attitude, Communication and Influence and Self-confidence and Self-belief, below are some development suggestions that you might find of use. To find resources on other areas see the Further Reading section at the back of the book which lists numerous books, articles and websites for each development area.

As you read through the list you will find that some areas appeal to you more than others. When you have completed the list, brainstorm any other ways in which you could develop in this area and note it in the section provided. Review your list and pick two or three areas that appeal to you most, and note these down so that you can build them into your Personal Development Plan.

You should have fun with this activity; this is an ideal time for you to try out new and different ideas and see yourself flourish and grow.

CREATIVITY AND INNOVATION

DEVELOPMENT SUGGESTIONS

- Give yourself permission to come up with new and novel ideas. Telling yourself that you are not creative becomes a self fulfilling prophecy. Enrol in a class that requires creative expression, e.g. painting, music, theatre. Make a point of visiting an art gallery or going to a play once in awhile.

- Surround yourself with creative people, ask them how they go about developing new ideas. What can you learn from their approaches? How do they view themselves? What do they enjoy about the creative process?

- Take a step back and ask yourself if there is a better way of doing something. Edward de Bono calls this a "Creative Pause". He suggests that you should take short pauses of no more than 30 seconds in our thinking and that we make it a habitual discipline. Set yourself the goal of coming up with at least one new idea each month. Record your successes.

- Shift your mindset and attitude. View problems as opportunities for improvement and then see it as the potential to come up with something new and novel.

- Go to your local book store and buy books on creativity or biographies of famous individuals who came up with creative solutions to problems. Edward De Bono's book *How to Have Creative Ideas* is an excellent book to encourage the skill of creativity and lateral thinking.

- Create an informal innovative task force whose sole purpose is to come up with fresh and new ideas. Use this task force to try out different approaches and methods.

- Look for connections. The more varied your interests, the greater the chance of cross-fertilisation, of combining two or more things that have not been combined before. Look for relationships between things that are not related.

- If you find that you are a slave to routine, for example, going to the same restaurant for lunch or travelling the same route to work each day, then vary it. Try something different. Breaking out of habits can begin to open you up to new and different possibilities.

- Keep a journal or notebook by your bed. Go to sleep with a question or a problem you want an answer to. Upon waking write down all the possible ideas that have come into your head or your dreams.

- Create the right frame of mind and environment to help you be more creative. Use some relaxation or mediation techniques to get both sides of your brain activated. Play soft music or go to a place which you find truly inspiring.

- Take one day every two months and go somewhere that truly inspires you. Bring a journal and write down whatever comes to you during that day. Don't force the process; just be present in the moment and see what comes up.

- Don't give up, creativity is not necessarily easy. Allow for plenty of mistakes and learn from them – it is part of the process.

USEFUL RESOURCES AND ACTIVITIES

Random Word Technique

Random word technique uses the generation of a random word to prompt creative thinking. The key to success is to focus on the exercise and not allow negativity to creep in as to the usefulness of this exercise. The process is as follows:

- Select a word from a magazine, a book or a newspaper.

- Link the random word to the topic that you are trying to generate ideas around. For example, if the topic you are trying to generate ideas around was gardens, and the random word was love, the linking idea would be to have gardens designed around the theme of love and thinking about the infrastructure and plants needed to create that environment.

- Generate ideas by replacing the topic problem with the random word and look at how you might apply the ideas behind the random word to your topic problem.

- You may be tempted to change the random word to something more suitable. DON'T. Go with the first choice even if it seems zany and way out.

Brainstorming

Encourage creative thinking within your working environment by holding brainstorming sessions. Clearly identify the topic or problem to be brainstormed and gather no more than 10 people to work on generating ideas collectively. The three basic rules are:

1. No criticism of ideas
2. All ideas are encouraged, no matter how odd
3. Participants should try to build on each other's ideas.

Keep the sessions to a maximum of 30 minutes and capture all the ideas on a flip-chart. After the session send the brainstorming notes to participants and ask them to identify their favourite idea and how it can be implemented.

Reverse Brainstorming

Reverse brainstorming uses a combination of brainstorming and reversal techniques. By combining both of these approaches you can generate even more creative solutions. Apply the same principles outlined above in holding brainstorming sessions to your reverse brainstorming session. Rather than asking, "how you can solve this problem", you begin by asking, "how you could create this problem", and rather than asking, "how you might get a successful outcome", you ask, "how could I go about getting an unsuccessful outcome". Having clearly stated the problem and reversed the questions as above, generate as many reverse solutions as possible. You can then reverse them again into possible solutions for the original problem or challenge.

Mind Mapping

Mind Mapping, developed by Tony Buzan, is an effective method for generating ideas by association. Write down you topic or theme in the centre of the page and draw branches from that centre and label them with sub-topics. Your topic might be leadership and the sub-topic might be communication, followers, integrity, passion and belief. From the sub-topics draw further thinner branches from these sub-topics and label these. Taking the sub-topic of communication you might write persuasion, influencing, listening, etc. Create as many levels as you feel are necessary.

Drawing

A good activity when you get stuck on a problem is to draw it. Keep the topic or issue to be addressed at the fore of your mind and then allow whatever comes up to be expressed on the page. This is not about artistic expression but about accessing the creative areas in your brain, so don't censor. Try to relax and allow your mind freedom of thought and expression. When you have finished drawing try to articulate what is on the page to someone else and capture the key points or ideas that seem worthwhile.

Edward de Bono's Six Thinking Hats

Brainstorming involves generating as many ideas as possible in relation to a particular issue or decision that needs to be made. This should provide you with a more comprehensive range of options to analyse. In brainstorming it is important to produce as many ideas as possible before evaluating any of them. It is also beneficial to encourage others to actively add to ideas that are presented. Edward de Bono's Six Thinking Hats is an excellent approach to thinking in different ways. You can use this to aid your own thinking or as part of a group thinking and brainstorming session. The Six Thinking Hats allow you to think in different ways by switching your thinking out of your usual track and using alternative approaches. The six hats are as follows:

White Hat

Looking at the current situation, you see what facts are available and where there might be gaps. Wearing this hat you look at what has happened in the past and try to learn from this to help you make decisions about the future.

Red Hat

Uses intuition, gut reaction and emotional response. When wearing this hat you think about your own and others' reactions based on gut feeling and intuition. It is not based on hard data and in fact might run contrary to what the facts are suggesting.

Black Hat

When you are wearing the black hat you take a negative or pessimistic stance and think about what might go wrong. You are focusing on the flaws and weaknesses of the idea or decison so that you can address or eliminate them.

Yellow Hat

The yellow hat is the opposite to the black hat. The yellow hat takes the optimistic viewpoint and helps you to see the benefits of what you are proposing or the decisions you are going to make. This type of thinking highlights the benefits and the value in what you are proposing so that you can enhance these areas and keep them to the fore of your mind in order to stay motivated.

Green Hat

This uses the creative processes to develop creative solutions to problems. It uses brainstorming techniques to come up with ideas which have no censure. Any of the methods described in this section will help you in the green hat space.

Blue Hat

When wearing the blue hat you are interested in controlling and directing the processes. When there is too much of a focus on Black Hat thinking you may direct the activity into Yellow Hat thinking and so on.

The benefits of using this approach with groups is that it allows people to look at problems and decisions from different perspectives and gives permission to be optimistic, critical, creative, etc. without creating disagreement or conflict.

Ideas or Actions You Can Take to Develop Creativity & Innovation

_____

_____

_____

_____

_____

_____

_____

ACTION ORIENTED

DEVELOPMENT SUGGESTIONS

- If you find that you are consistently saying you will get around to doing such and such thing – stop. Dive right in and tackle it rather than thinking and reflecting about what needs to be done.
- If you tend to be more reflective, surround yourself with people who are energetic and get things done. Try to learn from them as to how they manage to tackle the difficult tasks and get so much done.

- When you come up with good ideas or insights act on them immediately by talking to people who might be able to help you move them to the next stage.

- Push yourself to take on greater responsibilities and broaden your area of interests. Try and to involved in a number of different projects where you can contribute at a higher level than currently.

- Keep a diary of actions you have taken over a one month period. Think about how you go about turning plans into action. Do you tend to ponder too long over minor details? Are you too cautious, always striving for perfection? Do you worry about minor details that are really inconsequential? Whatever it is, identify what prevents you from taking action and put strategies in place to address them.

- Read about people who have achieved a lot and who are comfortable taking risks. What can you learn from them?

- Think about the qualities or characteristics that are needed to become more action oriented and list them on a sheet of paper. Where are you strong and what areas do you need to develop.?

- Think about situations or activities where you tend to be more action oriented. Are there aspects from these situations or activities that you can build on?

- Become proactive in getting involved in projects rather than waiting to be asked. If you spot something that needs to be done in your work setting, take the first step in making it happen.

- Set yourself goals that need to be achieved each week or month. Think about what might enable you to achieve them and what might block you. What strategies might you use to eliminate the blockers and enhance the enablers? Who might help you?

- Be proactive in developing your own initiative and motivational skills. Make a note of your behaviour when faced with problems or challenges, and watch out for signs that you might be procrastinating.

Useful Resources and Activities

Procrastination Strategies

We all know the scenario or the self-talk that goes with procrastination: "I know I need to do this but I don't want to, or I will do it later, or it is too beautiful a day to start on this now, or why do I always have to do x y or z and so on." There are many reasons why we procrastinate; by understanding what those reasons are you can then apply some useful strategies to deal with them. Some of the more common reasons as to why we procrastinate are listed below, but this list is by no means exhaustive you may have your own special procrastination reason which you might want to add below.

- You are not sold on the need to do the job or task; in other words, your motivational drivers aren't switched on or powered up. This may be because you think it is someone else's job to do whatever it is that needs doing, or that you think what needs to be done is a waste of time. If this is the case you need to come up with some good reasons as to why you should do this job or task or whatever it is you are putting off – you need to sell to yourself the benefits and rewards that will be gained on completion of the activity. Sometimes it is not a bad idea to list the repercussions of not doing what needs to be done; this can very quickly focus the mind into activity.

- Believe it or not, sometimes we don't do something because we are afraid of failing or even in some cases of succeeding. Check your self-talk and see if this is the case. Simply reprogram your thinking to redress the negativity or visualise your intended outcome and make it as pleasant as possible. See the rewards your gain from your success.

- You just don't want to do the task or job badly enough because there are other more enjoyable or pressing tasks or jobs that need to be done beforehand and which will provide more tangible rewards. The only way around this is to try to come up with good reasons why you should do the task or job and the ultimate consequences of not doing so. Think about the question Timothy Ferris asks in his book *The 4-hour Work Week*: "What is it costing you financially, emotionally and physically to postpone action? Don't only evaluate the potential downside of action. It is equally as important to measure the atrocious cost of inaction".

- Which brings us to another reason why we procrastinate: the task or job seems to overwhelmingly big or complex or we don't know enough about it. In this case, break the task or job into sizeable chunks. Do the aspects of the task you are comfortable and familiar with first, and either get more information on those aspects you are not so sure about or enlist some help or advice.

- Sometimes we put things off because we are just plain indecisive. Some people are more indecisive than others. The thought of having to make a decision makes them anxious because it closes down all the wonderful opportunities that are available. If this is the case, don't ponder, just do, and set yourself a deadline for making the decision.

- Some people set very high standards for themselves and consequently anything they do has to be of the highest standards. They won't let go until something is absolutely perfect. If this is the case, set yourself a deadline and have someone hold you accountable for keeping to that deadline.

- You just don't want to do the task because it is too unpleasant – blocked drains or toilets come to mind! You have two choices if this is the case: grin and bear it or get someone else to do it.

- If you haven't created the right environment for doing the task then start by getting your working space just right. Set time aside when you won't be distracted by other things and create a to-do list and stick to it. As personal development teacher Jim Rohn likes to say, "if you fail to plan, you plan to fail".

Speed Thinking

Can you think too much? According to Dr. Ken Hudson of The Speed Thinking Zone, we can get trapped in the cycle of paralysis by analysis and not get to the decision. He proposes the Two Minute challenge which is based on Ken Blanchard's book the *One Minute Manager*. Basically, you select a problem or issue and much like brainstorming you give yourself two minutes to come up with at least nine different responses without censuring. The basis of this exercise is that giving yourself such a short time frame makes you access the unconscious, intuitive mind and bypasses the analysis.

Speed Reading

Learn to speed read documents and books that are important to your work and where you are reading for understanding rather than detail. This involves:

- Chunking more words together and increasing the number of words that you read in a sentence. This will take some practice but will increase your reading speed. You should soften your eyes and scan the words rather than reading each word individually.

- Reduce the length of time that you spend on each word. You should push yourself to read each chunk (about 7 words) in less than 30 seconds. If you find that difficult, try to reduce 10 seconds at a time until you have mastered this goal.

- A lot of times when reading your concentration lapses and you find that you have to read back over a sentence. One technique that you can use to maintain concentration is to run a finger or a pen along the line as you read. Another is to have a question in your mind that you want an answer to. This will focus your mind more clearly on the content and will help with recall.

Activity Log

How much time do you spend on activities at work that are non-productive – checking out websites, shifting through junk e-mail, etc.? Many of us are not even conscious of what we do each day and when we are most productive. One way of checking how you spend your time is to complete an activity or record log of your day. You should keep this log over a one month period in order to build up a more complete picture of how you spend your time. On the log record the time, and the activities that you undertake each day and assess their value on a scale of 1 (Low Priority) to 5 (High Priority). Be as honest as you can. Note the activities as you do them on the log and when you change activities, note the duration of the previous activity and record the new one. At the end of each week, assess the percentage of time you are spending on each activity and whether it is a productive use of your time based on the rating. You may surprise yourself as to how much time you are spending on low value activities and by simply reducing or eliminating these activities will give you more time to take the necessary actions that are needed for you to be more effective. A sample log is outlined below to get you started.

Time	Activity	Rating	Duration	Actions to Increase/ Decrease

Ideas or Actions You Can Take to Improve Your Action Orientation

_____

_____

_____

_____

_____

_____

AUTHENTIC LEADERSHIP

DEVELOPMENT SUGGESTIONS

- Think about leaders you have experienced in the past and/or those that you have seen in the media. What qualities and characteristics do they possess? Is there anything you can learn from the way they have handled situations that you can apply to your own circumstances? Use the exercise in Useful Resources on Qualities of a Good Leader to help you do this.

- According to Genevieve Capowski: "Leaders are not born. Leaders are made, and they are made by effort and hard work." In other words, everyone has the basic seeds of leadership within them and how these are developed and cultivated will determine whether leadership qualities develop in an individual. Are you taking the time to develop and nurture the leadership seeds and qualities that are within you? Developing as a leader is a personal journey but some of the basic ingredients are about having a clear vision and the ability to influence and engage people with that vision. It is also about the flexibility to change and to be willing to take a stand, be courageous and challenge the status quo.

- Are there areas either within or outside your work context that you feel really passionate about? Where would you like to make a difference? This could be in relation to systems, processes, tasks or people. What talents could you utilise to make your passion a reality? If you knew you couldn't fail, what would you do differently? Write down your responses and discuss them with a colleague or friend.

- If you are leading a team or managing a group of people, it is important you have a good understanding of the strengths and development needs of your team as well as their motivators. When a team member feels appreciated and "looked after" by their leader they give of their best. Study some of the motivational theories that are in the literature like Maslow's Hierarchy of Needs, McGregor's Theory X and Theory Y and Hertzberg's Motivation Hygiene factors to gain a greater appreciation of what motivates people. Apply some of your findings.

- Leadership is all about cultivating relationships. How strong are the relationships that are important to you in achieving your goals? Do you need to spend some time building and developing these relationships? Draft up an action plan and follow it through.

- Develop a vision for your work area. Involve your team in pulling this vision together. Look at ways in which you might bring that vision to life.

- Develop a clear picture of your own value set and what you consider to be important. Are there any values which you have compromised recently? Are

125

you saying one thing and doing another? Leaders communicate their values and beliefs to others through their actions. If there are inconsistencies these need to be addressed as people don't follow you just on the basis of your authority but on your example as a role model.

- Are you clear on your strengths and development areas as a leader? Nobody is perfect or has the complete package, and we cannot please everyone all of the time, but having a clear sense of your own strengths and shortcomings and trying to address the latter is important in order to build your credibility as a leader. Do you regularly solicit feedback from others about both the positive and negative aspects of your style, or do you shy away from getting feedback? And when you do get negative feedback, how do you respond? Are you defensive or do you accept the feedback and reflect on what might be giving rise to that perception? If you don't regularly solicit feedback make a point of doing so. You may even decide to engage in a 360 degree process which was explained in Chapter Seven – Reality Testing.

USEFUL RESOURCES AND ACTIVITIES

Qualities of a Good Leader

This exercise is designed to help you to understand your personal mental map of the qualities and characteristics that you believe are important to be a good leader. A "mental map" is how you think about leadership in your head.

1. Think of one person you know who exemplifies really strong leadership qualities. It may be a person you have worked with or whom you have observed. This also can be a historical figure who may be alive or dead. They may not have a formal title of "leader"; rather, they may just have stepped up and taken a leadership role when it was required. Write their name below.

Person A: _____

2. Think of one person who demonstrates the opposite in leadership. Write their name below.

Person B: _____

3. Now compare A and B. What are the main differences? What was it that made A so good? Note down any key values and attributes that come to mind in distinguishing A from B.

4. Next list the key factors from all the above in approximate order of importance (the list does not have to be in precise order of importance, but some idea of what is most important would be of value).

5. Looking at some of those qualities and characteristics, in which areas are you strong and where is development needed?

Hersey-Blanchard's Situational Leadership

Are you aware of the different styles of leadership that you can employ depending on the requirements of the situation or the needs of the individual? According to Paul Hersey and Ken Blanchard, the most effective leaders adapt their style of leadership depending on the situation. They put together a model called Situational Leadership to explain the different styles that leaders use, focusing on four leadership styles that match the development needs of their people.

Leadership Style	Characteristics	Followers' Needs
Directive	Directing and instructing; setting clear objectives; following up regularly	Low Competence Low Confidence
Coaching	Listening, questioning and guiding; makes appropriate suggestions; holds back as much as possible from telling	Some Competence Some Confidence
Supportive	Listening, praising and building the confidence of the individual	High Competence Low Confidence
Delegating	Giving free reign; less need for support and praise, though occasional recognition is always important	High Competence High Commitment

Highest Level of Leadership

There is a belief in the wider business community that leadership at its highest level is more about serving others and giving back than about power and status. Jim Collins, in his book *Good to Great*, talks about the Level 5 leader who is characterised by an apparent dichotomy of personal humility and professional will. These are leaders who are modest yet willful, shy yet fearless. They embody a contradiction which makes them stand out in terms of their personalities, and the results they bring with them. Robert Greenleaf, the founding father of the concept of Servant Leadership, teaches that leadership is about leading by example, promoting community, and channeling power and authority towards helping others reach their potential, gain fulfillment and achieve well-being. Larry Spears, CEO of the Greenleaf Centre, builds on Greenleaf's idea and identifies ten characteristics of a servant-leader in his paper "On Character and Servant Leadership":

1. Listening

Greenleaf believes that servant-leaders should listen first and communicate second. Good ideas of others can be lost because leaders don't do enough listening and feel they have to fill the space by communicating. Also, servant-leaders must tune in and listen to both verbal and non-verbal signals and interpret what others are saying.

2. Empathy and Acceptance

The basic point is that you should nurture the essence of the individual and not reject them out of hand even though their behaviour may not be acceptable. Accepting people, though not necessarily all their actions, requires in Greenleaf's words, "a tolerance of imperfection".

3. Healing

Leadership is about healing the broken spirit of people and helping to make them whole again.

4. Awareness

Spears points out that "awareness broadens a leader's understanding of areas such as ethics, power and values". It is about broadening one's understanding beyond what is merely present so that the leader has a more holistic view of life.

5. Persuasion

This is about using influence rather than coercion in order to move things forward. It is about moving away from the autocratic style of leadership towards a relational style of leadership. It is about building consensus within a group.

6. Conceptualising

Speers believes that a leader must move beyond the day to day operational issues and be able to dream dreams and look to the future. This can be hard for leaders to do because they can be so caught up in the here and now but they must make the time to think about and plan for the future and create a vision of where they want to get to.

7. Foresight

Greenleaf calls foresight "the central ethic of leadership" and defines is as a "better than average guess about what is going to happen in the future". Good leadership therefore requires a detailed knowledge of the past, an understanding of the present and an intuitive grasp of the future.

8. Stewardship

The leader's role is first and foremost about serving the needs of others and holding in trust the future of the organisation or community for future generations. Spears uses Peter Block's definition (author of *Stewardship and the Empowered Manager*) as "holding something in trust for another".

9. Commitment to the Growth of People

Greenleaf would argue that people are more than the role they fulfil in organisations and that both their personal and professional growth should be harnessed. This may involve offering flexible working hours, finding them new positions if made redundant and providing necessary funds to their learning and development.

10. Building Community

Greenleaf said, "All that is needed to rebuild community as a viable life form for large numbers of people is for enough servant-leaders to show the way, not by mass movements, but by each servant-leader demonstrating his or her unlimited liability for a quite specific community-related group."

Speers concludes that interest in Servant Leadership is growing and that many of the companies named in *Fortune* magazine's annual listing of "The 100 Best Companies to Work For" espouse Servant Leadership as part of their corporate culture.

Waverley's Leadership Creed

Waverley Learning (UK) specialises in leading edge Leadership Programmes. Chris Blakely, Director of Waverley Learning, has succinctly captured the nature of effective leadership which is outlined below.

- Leadership cannot be conferred by some higher authority. It cannot be assumed or demanded, nor built on fear. It can only be bestowed.

- Leadership is always formed in relationship. A leader cannot lead without followers' consent. Each must offer something to the other.

- The aspiration to lead should arise from the desire to serve.

- Every follower wants to contribute to something meaningful. The greatest gift of the leader is a sense of purpose.

- The leader's role is not to convince others to share their vision but to live it, enabling others to discover their vision within themselves.

- The capacity to lead does not come from position or personality, but from self-knowledge and self-direction, from an understanding of one's particular strengths, motives, values and vision. Developing leadership capacity therefore requires inner work.

- While skills techniques may help the leader, they are no substitute for self-awareness. Leadership is not taught but self-developed.

- Leadership credibility is built on trust. Trust is given to those who demonstrate alignment between stated values and daily behaviours.

- Leadership does not diminish those who follow. It reveals and enhances their potential to become the complete human beings they are capable of.

- Leadership always creates a supportive environment for the development of other leaders.

- Leaders influence culture at every level of an organisation. Their day-to-day behaviours define its values. If you want to understand the nature of an organisation, watch the behaviour of the leaders.

Ideas or Actions You Can Take to Improve Your Leadership

_____

_____

_____

_____

_____

_____

POSITIVE ATTITUDE

Development Suggestions

- Think back to the last time a significant change was made in your work area. How did you react? Did you model a positive attitude to others? What effect did this have on their morale and enthusiasm for the change?

Development Options

- Listen to your internal voice over the course of a day and notice the type of messages you are repeating to yourself. You may even want to write them down so that you can get them out there and see them for what they really are. Are they mainly positive or negative? If you catch yourself playing negative messages to yourself such as "I can never do this" or "I am too stupid to learn anything new" turn these around by saying instead, "I am competent and capable" or "I can do anything I put my mind to".

- Work towards developing a more positive attitude. List three situations where you have felt very negative and then concentrate on all the possible benefits and advantages that could have been gained. Practise looking at opportunities as challenges rather than threats. Whenever you feel you are are taking a negative stance about a situation or issue, stop for a moment to look at the possible benefits and opportunities.

- Other people can impact on your level of energy and enthusiasm. Associate yourself with people who are more "upbeat and positive" rather than those who moan and complain all the time – you will be surprised at how much better you feel.

- When presented with a challenge or a new task, think about the beneficial outcomes first. Knowing that what you are doing is likely to make an improvement or deliver positive results can be highly motivating. Then think about how you will benefit from the work. Consider if it is an opportunity to:
  ◊ demonstrate your talents and potential, thereby enhancing your profile
  ◊ develop new skills, experience and/or knowledge
  ◊ work with interesting people/on interesting subjects
  ◊ take time out from your normal routine
  ◊ really stretch yourself and feel fulfilled.

- Choose to start your day on a positive note. Decide that you're going to have a good day, that you will enjoy the challenges ahead and working with your colleagues. Enter the office with a smile and a cheery "hello". It's amazing how much your personal demeanour can affect others.

- Allowing yourself to get stressed out will have a seriously negative effect on your enthusiasm. Learn to manage your stress levels – identify when your workload is having an adverse impact on your attitude and health, and do something about it.

- In the workplace it's important to be able to turn your negativity into positivity in order to achieve your goals, overcome obstacles and get through the difficult times. Below are some ways in which you can turn your negativity into positivity:

◊   be the one who focuses on the good rather than the bad

◊   come into work in a good mood

◊   be enthusiastic about new tasks and problem solving

◊   have a positive impact on people around you

◊   enjoy yourself in the process.

- Make sure that you take care of all aspects of your being – your physical health (get rest, eat well, cut down on addictive substances); your mental health (be open to new experiences and challenges, stretch your thinking and try to stay positive); your emotional health (give yourself treats) and your spiritual self (take time out to meditate and reflect; think about what is important to you).

Useful Resources and Activities

Observing Your Self-Talk

Your internal voice helps navigate you through life and in that respect it is useful, but if you don't control or watch what you are saying it can limit you in what you want to achieve. Most people are continually giving themselves suggestions for bad feelings, inaction and a lack of confidence and then wonder why they feel so bad. Over the next week, whenever you catch yourself thinking something negative about yourself, say, "DELETE THAT THOUGHT".

Take a few moments to think of some of the negative suggestions you have habitually given yourself in the past, things like:

"I'll never be able to do that."

"I hate my job and where I work."

"I am terrible at giving presentations."

For each statement, turn it around to come up with its positive opposite.

"I'm a naturally confident person."

"I am moving towards the job of my dreams."

"All my talents are being used to full effect."

"I give excellent presentations."

When you catch yourself falling into the old negative self-talk trap, turn around what you are saying into something positive.

Ten Ways to Help Manage your Stress

Steps	Commitment to Action
1. **Nourish Your Body**. Eat and drink sensibly, and give up smoking and other bad habits. We tend to indulge in food, drink and other bad habits like smoking when under stress. Caffeine, alcohol, sugary foods and nicotine abuse may seem to reduce stress, but they actually add to it. Nourish your body and give it the gift of good wholesome food, fresh fruit and vegetables and plenty of water.	
2. **Assert Yourself and Know Your Limitations.** Often we find that rather than asserting what we really want we just go with the flow in order to keep the peace. You do not have to meet others' expectations or demands all of the time. It's okay when appropriate to say "No." Knowing your limitations and boundaries allows you to have a healthy respect for yourself, whilst at the same time acknowledging and respecting the boundaries of others.	
3. **Get Plenty of Exercise.** Exercise actually releases positive chemicals called endorphins which are a natural substance that help you feel better and more positive. Aim for 30 minutes at least three to four times a week. The form of exercise you take doesn't always have to be strenuous. Yoga, for example, is a gentle form of exercise which is excellent in building strength and stamina while relaxing the mind and the body.	
4. **Learn to Relax and Take Power Naps.** Your mind, just likes your body, needs regular exercise if it is to serve you well. Visualisation, meditation and power naps are excellent ways to condition and fine-tune the mind. You don't need to do anything special in order to meditate; just find a quite place to relax and focus on an object or your breathing. Like exercise you need to start gently (two to three minutes in the morning and evening is a good place to start) and continue to build your practice until you can manage 30 minutes a day without much effort. If you are interested in learning more, there are many different techniques and programmes available online.	

Steps	Commitment to Action
5. **Laugh Often and Hard.** Laughter is a great remedy for lifting your mood and releasing stress. Research has shown that changing our very physiology like our facial expression from a frown into a smile can change our mood from one of negativity to one of positivity. Laughter has also been found to reduces stress hormones including adrenaline, cortisol and epinephrine. Sigmund Freud, in his book *Jokes and Their Relationship to the Unconscious,* describes laughter as the body's way of safely releasing anxiety, aggression, fear and anger.	
6. **Take Control and Censor What You Listen to.** Too often we tune into the radio or pick up the paper as a way of relaxing only to find that the bad news and negativity increase our stress levels. Control what you listen to or read, switch now and again to listening to uplifting music or listening to self-help DVDs as you drive to work.	
7. **Treat Yourself.** Massages are a great way to relieve stress. When we become stressed we tend to hold the stress as tension points in different parts of the body, typically our necks, shoulders and back. An experienced masseur can gently work out the tension spots and bring you back to a wonderful sense of well-being.	
8. **Live in the Now.** Most of us are either stuck in the past with all its pain and hurt or living in the future with all its fears and uncertainty. Few of us focus on the present, the NOW. Practice reconnecting with what you are currently doing and try to keep your mind focused on really enjoying that activity. Bring all your senses into play – hearing, seeing, smelling, touching, etc. – and relish the current moment.	
9. **Know What is Important.** Get reacquainted with what is important to you – your values and your beliefs. Learn to live by these values and beliefs and you will find that your life will be in better balance.	

Steps	Commitment to Action
10. **Believe in Yourself.** Have a healthy sense of balance about who you are and what you have accomplished. Learn to genuinely love who you are and remind yourself often of what you do well. Accept that we all have flaws and make mistakes – it is part of the journey that we are all on.	

Ideas or Actions You Can Take to Improve Your Positive Attitude

_____

_____

_____

_____

_____

_____

BUILDING RELATIONSHIPS

DEVELOPMENT SUGGESTIONS

- Speak with other people who you consider to be particularly effective in building relationships. Discuss with them how they have gone about building those relationships. What lessons have they learned and what have been some of the tangible and intangible benefits? Also discuss with them if there are any techniques that they have found to be particularly effective.

- It is important to note that not all relationships are reciprocal and that you might consider that you are doing all the "giving" and getting little in return. Again, it is worth discussing with others how they have effectively dealt with such issues.

- Think about people who you normally don't mix with and who are different to you in their work, their interests and their social outlets. Take the opportunity to get to know them and use it to broaden your understanding of people.

- Practice building social skills by trying the following:
  - ◊ Be aware of the atmosphere of a conversation, and match the other person's posture. Pay attention to how they move or remain still. Then, gradually adapt your positions so that they match or mirror theirs.
  - ◊ Match their tone of voice. Vocal tone is comprised of pitch (high or low), speed (fast or slow), and volume (loud or soft). If those around you are speaking in quieter or more boisterous tones, do the same.
- Build rapport by harmonising your behaviors and actions with others. Take steps to find a shared or common interest or a shared commitment and enthusiasm for accomplishing a goal.
- Encourage open authentic communication. To build trust share your own thoughts, ideas and feelings. Don't allow it to be all one way traffic, and follow up on your commitments - do what you say and say what you mean. Inconsistency in your thoughts, words or actions can create a strong sense of distrust that can ultimately destroy any rapport that exists in a relationship. If you can't keep your promises, discuss and develop mutually agreeable alternatives.

Useful Resources and Activities

Building Effective Relationships that Work

Relationships can often seem like fragile things – especially in the workplace where they are often built and destroyed by the actions we take. However, as Nick Heap explains, by underpinning those relationships with a few simple principles, they can grow into something secure and lasting. In the next two sections he highlights four things that can help build relationships and four things that can destroy relationships.

Aspects that Build Effective Relationships

1. **At least one party should decide the relationship is important**. Deciding that your relationship with someone is important means that you will invest time and energy to understand the other person's needs and you will be more inclined to deal with anything that gets in the way. It's easier if the other person thinks it's important too, but not essential.

2. **Learn to listen effectively, and without judging**. Effective and non-judgemental listening will help you to understand the other person. When someone listens to you, both your own sense of worth and the worth of the listener increases. Judging another person almost always creates distance and defensiveness.

3. **Meet people informally, so they feel comfortable raising issues that are important to them**. Most people feel more relaxed in informal settings. If you are intending to meet with someone with the specific purpose of developing your relationship with that person, think about holding the meeting in a setting in which he or she will feel comfortable.

4. **Develop a culture whereby people can express their feelings.** We create relationships by sharing thoughts and feelings. When we express happiness, joy, contentment, anger, irritation, sadness or fear we feel more vulnerable, but we can also feel more connected. Organisational cultures that encourage people to connect can generate a passionate commitment to achieve wonderful things together.

Aspects that Get in the Way of Building Effective Relationships

1. **A history of mistrust or stereotyping**. We get a great deal of misinformation about people who are different to ourselves. There is often more difference between the members of a group than between groups. If ever we think "All _____ are like that" then we are stereotyping. This causes destruction in relationships; everyone wants to feel unique. When stereotyping is endemic, consistent mistreatment or oppression of one group by another is common, which in turn reinforces people's negative feelings that can, understandably, colour their attitudes.

2. **Blaming the other party for a difficult relationship**. Blaming another person or group is usually futile. It creates distance and defensiveness, and does not help the relationship develop. If you are not happy about a relationship, it is more useful to think about what you need to do, or not to do, to make it better. You can change your behaviour much more easily than you can persuade others to change theirs.

3. **Focusing on the task and excluding the feelings and needs of others**. People have feelings and they bring those feelings to work. Well run organisations harness those feelings and help people use their energy, joy and laughter to good effect. People are not machines; if they are treated with respect and understanding, if their feelings are listened to, they will want to give more and work better together.

4. **Unclear objectives, roles and expectations of each other**. If we don't know what we want from each other, misunderstandings are inevitable and the relationship will suffer.

Effective Techniques for Building Relationships

Method 1: Active Listening

Here one party summarises in their own words what they hear the other person say and the feelings underlying it. They then give feedback to this person. The process continues until the talker is sure the listener understands. Then the roles are reversed.

Method 2: Taking Turns to Help Each Other

Each person has a turn describing an issue, idea or problem. The first acts as consultant and helps the second to arrive at a solution. At the end of the turn, the person being helped gives the consultant feedback on what the other did that helped. Then the roles are reversed. This technique is an economical and effective way to give and receive help and build good relationships at the same time. It will work if you take turns. Then both people feel good about giving and getting useful help.

Method 3: Helping Contracts

On the left-hand side of a sheet of paper, write down a list of "things I can do to help you". Then, on the right-hand side, write a list of "things you could do to help me". Invite the other person to add to both lists. Discuss the results and work on the changes.

Method 4: Process Review

Half-way through a meeting, ask each participant to say how they think the meeting is going. You can use phrases like: "What is good about the way we are working together?" and "How can we improve the second half of our meeting?" If this is difficult to do during the discussion, ask similar questions at the end of any significant meeting.

Method 5: Joint Projects

Identify projects that require participation from two or more groups. Involve members of these groups in the planning of the project, and make sure you discuss with them how the meetings are going and how to improve them.

Method 6: Joint Activities

Creating something together can be an excellent way of building relationships between groups. This is especially true when the activity requires talents, organisational ability, social skills and contacts, which you cannot predict from group membership.

For more information on this or other articles visit www.nickheap.co.uk.

Ideas or Actions You Can Take to Improve on Building Relationships

_____

_____

_____

_____

_____

_____

SELF-CONFIDENCE AND SELF-BELIEF

DEVELOPMENT SUGGESTIONS

- Be willing to take risks and go the extra mile to achieve better things. It's natural to put up barriers to ideas and new tasks when you feel you might fail. Before saying to yourself, "I can't do this", think about what is actually being said or asked of you and ask some questions to check your understanding. You might then be able to influence the extent of your role or realise that it's not quite as complicated as it first seemed.

- Stop comparing yourself with others. You'll always find people who are better than you at some things, and others who are worse. The only meaningful comparison is between you as you used to be, and you as you are now. If you lapse into thinking "I'm not as ... (attractive/clever/athletic etc) as ...", stop it. Tell yourself, "I'm a wonderful, amazing being. I'm good enough, and I'm grateful for it."

- List situations which you would like to handle more appropriately, e.g. managing upwards, getting your point across at meetings, not becoming overly defensive with people. Chose a colleague or close friend who will support you in dealing with these situations. Develop tactics to deal with these situations and role-play your response before trying it in real life. Remember, Rome wasn't built in a day so congratulate yourself on any small wins you may have made.

- The way you view yourself and your abilities can have a major impact on the way you present yourself to others. Doubting yourself and worrying what other people think of you is self-destructive. Be aware, and make others aware, of your talents by maximising the opportunities to demonstrate them. Think and talk about what you are, not what you're not.

- What aspects of yourself do you find most difficult to accept? Are there times or situations when you find it harder to be self-accepting than others? Jot down what stops you giving yourself permission to be as you are. Then write down a statement affirming those aspects you have difficulty with. Paste this on your fridge or computer and affirm those aspects of yourself on a regular basis.

- Everyone makes mistakes so become comfortable with yours. Admit your mistakes and vow to learn from them. Think about a time when you have been confronted with a difficult situation which you didn't handle as well as you would like. Who was involved? What was the situation? What did you learn and what would you do differently? Write out what you want to change about yourself or work on as a result of your reflection. Confide in a trusted other who will give you honest feedback on how well you are achieving your goal.

- Learn from constructive feedback but don't dwell on mistakes. Make sure that you focus on the present moment; worrying about the past and fretting about the future will only drain your energy and erode your self-confidence. Write down how much time you spend thinking about the past, present and future in any one day. Is this in perspective?

- Use the exercises in this workbook to take stock of where you are, think about where you want to go, and get yourself in the right mindset for your journey and commit to sticking with it. List the things you are particularly strong at and put them down on a piece of paper titled "Achievement Log". Look at this list often and enjoy the successes you have already had.

- Do what you believe to be right, even if others mock or criticise you for it. How often in the past has your behaviour been governed by what other people think? Have you compromised your beliefs or values to accommodate others, not because it is the right thing to do but because you wanted to please them? Think about strategies you might use to handle these situations the next time around.

USEFUL RESOURCES AND ACTIVITIES

Eight Qualities of a Self-confident Person

Self-confidence is freedom from doubt, faith in yourself and in your abilities, self-esteem, and the inner conviction that you can suceed at any task or action. It is the mark of inner strength. Self-confidence is extremely important in almost every aspect of our lives, yet so many people struggle to really find it. Self-confidence can be developed and built up over time – it just requires dedication and commitment. There are small things you can do each day to build your confidence. Below are some qualities you may want to begin to develop in your life to build your confidence and self-esteem.

1. Self-confident people are not perfect and they know it. However, they don't dwell on their inadequacies but focus instead on their strengths. When they make a mistake they own up, apologise and move on. They don't allow themselves to fall into the victim mode, nor do they allow others to put them in that box.

2. Self-confident people are open to feedback and adjust their behaviour if they feel it is appropriate. They don't shy away from the hard truths about themselves, seeing growth and development as a journey of experience and learning. They are also more open to taking risks and trying something new because they are not afraid of looking stupid . Think about the traits or qualities of a self-confident person, preferably someone you know. How do you compare in relation to some of the qualities you have identified? Are you hiding some of your insecurities behind an abrasive manner and are you open to feedback?

3. Self-confident people focus outward on others, and are not self-absorbed and constantly looking inwards. They believe in give and take and are open to the views of others and welcome their input. At the same time, they are secure in their own beliefs and are not easily swayed by others. They do no run with the foxes and hunt with the hounds. Their ideas do not fluctuate based on what others deem to be important.

4. Self-confident people know what they believe and what is important to them and they live by these principles and values. When was the last time you really thought about what you know and gained from life's experience? Maybe you could start recording some of your memoirs or writing down some of your ideas or thoughts? Keeping a daily journal is a great way of gaining perspective on your life experience, giving you insights into where you have grown and developed and what you have learnt about yourself.

5. Self-confident people are not pushy and arrogant; they don't need to force their views and beliefs on others because they are comfortable with what they believe to be true and are confident enough to allow other people to hold opposing views and beliefs.

6. Self-confident people are optimistic about obtaining a positive outcome. They don't allow blocks or negativity to get in their way. If they do encounter a setback, they quickly dust themselves off and look for a way around the obstacle. They have the confidence to ask for help if necessary or to learn a new skill in order to succeed.

7. Self-confident people don't torture themselves, and ultimately those close to them, by trying to be the best at everything. They cut themselves enough slack

so that they can enjoy life. They don't set the bar so high in every area of their life that it becomes painful and difficult.

8. Self-confident people are grateful for what they do have, and they make a practice of reminding themselves of all the good things in their life. Next time you are out for a walk mentally go through all the things you are grateful for in your life – family to friends, health, possessions, work, etc. It is a sure fire way to lift your moods and spirits and to give you more zest for life. Being positive and energetic builds your confidence and attracts people to you.

Ideas or Actions You Can Take to Improve Your Self-confidence and Self-belief

_____

_____

_____

_____

_____

Again, for suggestions for research in other development areas see the comprehensive list of resources in the Further Reading section at the back of the book.

DEVELOPMENT PLANNING

How to Put All of This Information Together

By now you should be in a position to integrate what you have learned about your strengths, development needs and career aspirations to form a concrete plan for the months ahead. However, it will not be possible to tackle everything immediately. Remember, it is better to meet realistic goals than to fail on overly ambitious ones.

The goal of this section is for you to optimise the use of your time and resources. To do so, you will need to ensure that you are developing the areas that will:

• Have a positive impact on your performance

• Give you greater personal satisfaction in your career and your life in general.

Review the summary results of all the exercises you have completed so far. Ensure that your goals and plans don't conflict with your Exploring You section. For example, you might have indicated on the Life Style Choices Exercise that you want to spend more time with your family. Unfortunately, to achieve your career goal may require working ten hours a day.

Similarly, you may have identified a high need to be the expert as part of the Personality Profiling, but to achieve your goal requires you to manage others and move away from your area of expertise. Be aware of dual conflicts and of the trade offs that may be involved in reaching your goal.

Based on the summary results of all exercises, try to determine your top two or three priorities, what you would like to achieve in your career and development in the future. Try thinking between one to three years down the line. Write your answers in the boxes below.

Q.1. What are the top three priority areas for your career and development, based on your own assessment and feedback from your respondent group?

_____

_____

_____

_____

Q.2. What development ideas will help you address those priorities?

_____

_____

_____

_____

_____

Q.3. What are your key talents and strengths that you want to enhance and use more effectively to help you move closer to your goals? In what other ways could you use these talents?

_____

_____

_____

_____

_____

Career and Development Planning Worksheet

Goal (complete a worksheet for each goal)

Specific Development Goal:

_____

_____

_____

_____

What Will Be Different?

_____

_____

_____

_____

How Will You Benefit?

_____

_____

_____

_____

_____

Strategies for Development

(Try to choose three to four different strategies such as training, mentoring, expanding your current role, reading, shadowing others, etc.)

Development Options

Strategy One

Specific Goal	Specific Actions

Strategy Two

Specific Goal	Specific Actions

Strategy Three

Specific Goal	Specific Actions

Moving Forward Themes

Key Things Holding Me Back
Actions to Help Me Overcome the Things Holding me Back

Key Things Pushing Me Forward
Actions to Help Me Make More of the Things Pushing Me Forward

Part Four

Finding the Job
You Love

Developing Your Vision

Building Your Brand

Promoting and Selling YOU

Creating the Mindset for Success

9

Developing Your Vision

"Your vision will become clear only when you can look into your own heart. Who looks outside, dreams, who looks inside, awakens." – Carl Jung

INTRODUCTION

Possibly now more than ever you need to have a clear vision for the future which will sustain you and keep you on track. A vision provides both a directional and a motivational function. It permits you to dream the impossible and to step out into the unknown with confidence, and it breaks down the barriers of what is achievable and realistic and opens up a whole new avenue of opportunities.

All successful CEOs and organisations believe in the importance of having a clear vision because they know it is the glue that holds their strategy together. It provides them with the framework to accomplish their goals, to benchmark their success along the way and to change course if they are losing sight of what is important. Having a vision is a tremendous personal power that we all possess and an important prerequisite to achieving great things.

Champion athletes are another group who use visualisation as a strategy to enhance their performance. They imagine winning an event over and over again until their mind and body know exactly what it is they want to do. Michael Schumacher, one of the world's greatest formula one racing drivers, mentally rehearsed every race beforehand. And golfer Jack Nicklaus said, "I never hit a shot, not even in practice, without having a very sharp in focus picture of it in my head."

A vision is a commonly understood and accepted sense of where you will be in the future and what you will be doing. It is a critical first step and one that will guide and sustain you through some of the difficult terrain that you may encounter along the way. It should be something that will stretch you, will take time to reach and that when reached will make you stand back in awe of the accomplishment. A vision that is worth achieving will motivate you to invest whatever amount of time, energy, money and effort that is necessary to make it a reality.

Envisioning your future is the most important activity you'll ever engage in as career seekers, as professionals and as human beings. Completing the visioning exercise will help to enhance your career prospects and your job search targets, and will give these areas much greater purpose and meaning.

At this point in the workbook you should have a pretty good insight into:

- Your skills and talents
- Your ideal job and work environment
- The strengths that you can call on to achieve your goals
- The skills, knowledge and behaviours you will need to develop further
- What is important to you as a person and where you would like to create more balance.

You can use these insights to help formulate your vision, but don't be restricted to just focusing on your career. Your career is only one aspect of your life. In the same way that organisations have many departments, you too have many different departments within yourself of which your career is but one. For example, if part of your vision is to retire early so you can travel then you may want to focus on a career that will provide you with the opportunity to earn a substantial amount of money in a short period of time. Or if part of your vision is to set up your own business as a freelance consultant, you might want to focus on job opportunities that build your reputation in your specialist area and provide you with a strong networking base for the future.

Remember: your vision should inspire, excite and motivate you towards higher goals and aims, so be expansive. It should not be based only on current reality and what is possible and achievable. It should be timeless, not time-bound, based on possibilities and dreams – so go ahead and dream!

The exercises below will help you begin the process of developing your vision.

Step 1 – Visualisation Exercise

In order to do this exercise it is important to engage both your conscious and your subconscious mind. You are at your creative best when your mind is in what is called the "Alpha" state. Alpha is the state of deep relaxation – the state you feel right before you drop off to sleep or upon gently waking up in the morning. Meditation is one way to get your mind into Alpha mode. When you get in a deep meditative state, you are in Alpha cycle. Below is a script, adapted from Paul Roland's book *How to Meditate,* that you can have a friend read out or you can record to play back to yourself. Alternatively, there are many great meditation and visualisation DVDs on the market which you can use. The important point is to create a state of readiness in your mind for creating your future. So let's begin.

Relaxation Script

Make yourself as comfortable as possible, switch off the phone and give yourself some time and space to do the following activity. I am going to take you on a mental journey to get you into a place of calm relaxation and help you access and synchronise both aspects of the brain. When we are truly relaxed, and when we programme and visualise our dreams and our future, our subconscious mind gets immediately to work to make those dreams a reality.

Close your eyes and begin by focusing on your breathing. Inhale as deeply as you can and when you reach the top of your breath hold for a count of three and then exhale to a count of five letting the air out in a long, slow breath. Pause before taking the next breath and sense the stillness and silence of that moment. Take another deep breath, pause again and sink deeper into stillness and silence. Now take regular breaths, pausing for a few moments as you inhale and exhale. Each time you do this try to immerse yourself in those moments when there is no movement in the body and no sound, not even of your own breathing.

Establish a regular rhythm then, when you are suitably relaxed, imagine that you are lying on a small rowing boat and you are drifting on the calm blue water in a quite lagoon. You can hear the gentle ebb and flow of the water as it splashes gently against the side of the boat. All is calm and relaxing, and except for the occasional bird song in the distance, a wonderful silence envelopes you. You are completely and utterly relaxed. In the silence between the calls of the birds you catch the rustle of leaves on the far bank as a cooling breeze sweeps in from the sea. With each call of the birds you are becoming more and more relaxed. The sound is so small that you have to strain to hear it and as you do you sink deeper and deeper into a profound state of relaxation.

You trail your hand over the side of the boat and you can feel the coolness of the water against the tips of your fingers. You make small splashing sounds and you smile quietly to yourself as you relish this time alone. You feel the healing rays of the warm sun on your body and in the background there is a cooling breeze which gently cresses your skin. You sink deeper and deeper into relaxation.

You can see the blue almost cloudless sky above and you catch a glimpse of an exotically colourful bird flying overhead. Time has no meaning as you drift along and all your cares just ease away. The sun sparkles on the water like diamonds and you close your eyes to avoid the glare.

As you look from bank to bank you are dazzled by the vivid colours of the tropical plants and you inhale their intoxicating scents and smells deeply. You are truly in a magical place, out of the ordinary and you simply exist to experience and enjoy the sights, sounds, smells and tastes of this secluded world. A bubble of deep contentment flows through your body as you float away as if on a cloud.

The boat carries you to a small inlet where you can see a beach with soft white sand, lined with beautiful palm trees that sway gently with the breeze. You can see in the distance that a feast has been laid out for you and for the first time you feel a small grumbling in your stomach. You get out of the boat and you feel the lush warm sand under your feet. You dig your toes deeper into the sand enjoying the sensation.

You eat and drink your fill, and when you are satisfied you make your way back to the boat and you drift off into a peaceful relaxed state as you make your way back to your water bungalow. As you emerge back at your bungalow you become aware of your surroundings, feel the weight of your body on the chair or floor or bed and slowly open your eyes.

Step 2 – Establishing Your Vision For Your Life

Now, having done some form of relaxation exercise and given yourself some time and privacy, think about and answer the questions below. This is free form writing or brainstorming, and remember that the principle behind brainstorming is to write without censoring your thoughts, so just keeping writing, don't worry about spelling and punctuation and if the ideas dry up, repeatedly write the word and ... and ... and on the page until the ideas flow again and you are sure that you have exhausted all of them. Spend about four or five minutes on each question. Remember, this is just a draft, not your final version.

1. Imagine it is 10 years into the future; see yourself at that point in time. What have you accomplished? Where are you living? What are your relationships like? Where are you working? What are your work colleagues like?

_____

_____

_____

_____

_____

2. What legacy would you like to leave behind? What would you like people to say about you?

_____

_____

_____

_____

_____

3. What aspects or qualities of your life do you currently enjoy and couldn't do without?

_____

_____

_____

_____

_____

4. What qualities do you value in yourself and others?

_____

_____

_____

_____

_____

5. If you couldn't fail what would you be doing right now?

_____

_____

_____

_____

_____

Step 3 – Your Vision Statement

Leave your writing aside for a few moments and then come back to it. Look at what you have written and circle key words and phrases. Having done that, write a two or three line statement that captures your vision for your life. This is an initial draft and something you will continue to work on over time. Carry it with you and add or delete as necessary. It will grow and develop as time goes on as you grow into your vision and it reflects who you truly are. As Jim MacNeish says in *Emerging Light*: "We believe people do not really change – they just become more of who they really are. People can spend a lifetime in the question 'who am I?' And rightly so. The process of becoming who you are created to be is a lifelong journey. But rather than getting stressed over having to find an answer, we need to find peace in the enquiry."

When you have finalised your vision statement write it down, cut it out and put it in a place where you can see it on a regular basis. This will act as your guiding light for the future and against which you will develop your concrete actions to make this vision a reality. After a period of time you should review your vision statement to check that it still meets with your life objectives and needs.

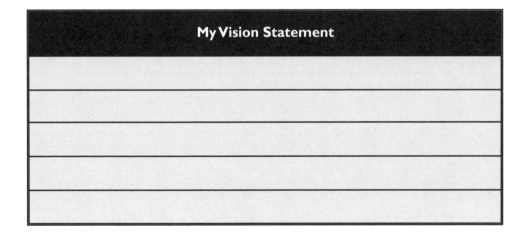

My Vision Statement

Step 4 – Taking Action for Success

On the basis of the vision statement you have just written, brainstorm as many goals as possible that you would like to achieve over the next three years and which would help you move towards your vision. Use your knowledge from the preceding exercises to help you in this regard, but don't just limit yourself to what you already know. Your goals don't all have to be related to your career. Think about what you would like in your personal life in terms of maybe relationships or health. Life issues will have an impact on the career that you will ultimately choose; alternatively, you may look for a career that will satisfy these issues. Either way, you should let your mind flow; don't censure anything that comes to mind but write everything down. Have as many stretching goals that appeal to you as possible. Really challenge yourself and your imagination.

Goals for the Next Three Years

Goals	
1.	11.
2.	12.
3.	13.
4.	14.
5.	15.
6.	16.
7.	17.
8.	18.
9.	19.
10.	20.

From your list of goals pick your top seven that you want to work on over the next three years. These goals should be areas that you feel most strongly about and if achieved would bring you a great deal of satisfaction.

Top Seven Goals – Three Years

1.
2.
3.
4.
5.
6.
7.

Step 5 – Programming for Success

Next we need to programme for success and let your subconscious mind get to work on your behalf. Every thought that reaches your conscious mind gets transferred to your subconscious mind for filing. This becomes your "hard drive", and your conscious mind draws on it for all the decisions you make. This is done automatically, and often without effort or deliberation. Your subconscious mind doesn't question, argue or doubt. It accepts the reality of the situation as it is presented. It responds very well to imaginary scenarios as it cannot tell the difference between what is real and what is imagined. So when you affirm things like, "I am in perfect health", it works to make that true. The more real you make things, and the stronger you imprint them, the faster your subconscious mind can make them come true in reality. So what you want to do is involve as many of your senses as you can and make them as colourful and as bold as possible.

Remember that in step one we said that the best way to get your creative juices flowing was to get your mind into an "Alpha" state. Similarly, the best time to programme your subconscious mind is when it is in Alpha state, so before you programme your subconscious mind using the script below, get your mind back into Alpha mode by doing the following simple exercise.

Exercise 1: Getting into a Meditative Alpha State

First, get in a relaxed position, either sitting or lying down, close your eyes, and begin breathing deeply. Breathe in through your nose and as you reach the top of your breath hold it for a count of three, and exhale out your mouth counting to five. Do this two or three times and then allow your breathing to return to normal and continue to take slow, steady deep breaths.

Begin counting backwards from 50, with each exhalation. Clear your mind of outside thoughts, and just concentrate on the next number. If stray thoughts come into your mind, just notice they are there, then release them and go to your next number. You will be in a deep alpha state by the time you get to one. You now can start programming your subconscious mind using the following script. Either have it recorded, memorised or have a friend read it to you.

Exercise 2: Creating Your Future Now

Taking the goals and the dreams you wish to achieve, imagine it is a year in the future and you have had the best year of your life. See, feel, hear, notice what is going on. What has happened in your career, your life, your relationships? What goals have you achieved? What progress have you made towards them? How have you changed? Who is present? How are they supporting you?

Now make a picture of your ideal future where you are living out all your dreams and goals in a way that doesn't seem possible now. See yourself in that future looking really positive and happy. Design your ideal scene now. What does it look like? Who is there? Where are you? Which successes are you most proud of? What aspects make you the happiest person alive?

Now mentally walk forward into a time when this future is really happening. See, feel, hear, notice what is going on. Make sure it is really bold, bright and colourful. Really allow yourself to enjoy experiencing it fully. What will it be like to have everything you want?

Allow your imagination to call up a resource that will help you achieve your dreams, e.g. tenacity, courage, integrity. When you have identified the resource, remember a time when you had that resource in abundance. Allow this resource to magnify and become powerful and see yourself really changing as you receive that resource.

Now allow your imagination to call in someone who will help you achieve your dreams, and who will act as your guide or mentor. They may be real or imagined, dead or alive. Trust your imagination to bring to mind who that might be. When they are present, listen to any advice they may have for you. Is there anything you want to ask? If so, ask it now and listen for their response. Allow what they have to say to affect you.

Bring to mind again your ideal scene with your new found resource and mentor. Take your dreams from that ideal scene and place each one in a balloon. Give each dream a colour and when you have done that gently blow those balloons out into the universe, knowing that they will come back to you with rich abundance.

Finally, link your ideal scene through a succession of pictures back to the present you. These should get successfully smaller as they link back to your present state. Look now at the pictorial map you have created from your present to your future. Your unconscious mind has now got a road map it can use as a guide to your future dreams and desires.

Step 6 – Formulating Action Plans

On the following pages you will find a sample of action plans. The action plans have been designed to help you succeed in meeting your goals and objectives including your career goals. Use the following steps to help you complete your required number of action plans.

1. Take each of your top seven goals identified earlier one at a time and write its name in the "Area" box.

2. Next you need to arrive at a number of specific objectives for that broad goal or heading. It may be that each goal or heading will require effort on more than one front and as such may require two or three objectives. For example, if your broad goal is to become Marketing Director in two to three years, this might mean two things: "getting involved in more strategic marketing activities" and "gaining greater visibility with the senior management by promoting your creative ideas".

3. When it comes to setting objectives, make sure they are SMART, i.e.:
   - **S**pecific
   - **M**easurable
   - **A**ction oriented
   - **R**ealistic
   - **T**ime bound.

4. For instance, taking the example of building relationships with key senior managers, a SMART objective would be: "To build a network of regular contacts (at least one from each business or funcational area) before the end of the financial year. Relationships must be two way and with at least monthly contact."

5. Once you have set your objectives, you need to identify activities that will facilitate your development. Using the Development Activity Menu for ideas, select a manageable number of activities that will meet your needs. Remember, this is

only one of a number of action plans so be mindful of the overall time commitment you are making.

6. Next you need to consider potential obstacles to your success. What are the things that might prevent you from completing these activities?

7. Now try to brainstorm some solutions to these obstacles. This section should act like an early warning system. You will now be more likely to notice any obstacle occurring and ready to take corrective action quickly.

8. The next section of the form requires you to articulate a number of measures of success. Try to find a quantitative measure if possible. For instance, if you are aiming to develop your confidence in negotiating, a quantitative measure of success would be the number of times that you succeeded in negotiations, i.e. your "hit rate".

9. Achieving your goals can be aided by having help and support from people who can guide you and sustain your motivation. Try to think of people who could help you on the way. They may act as an expert coach, a mentor to keep you focused, or simply a buddy to keep you interested and on track. In general, people are better at sticking to deadlines if someone else is relying on them. This is the basis of the buddy system where two or more people with a common aim agree to complete various tasks to a common deadline.

10. Finally, set some review dates.

You can use these action plans in any way that suits you. Within the career structure they can be used for learning and development purposes, for finding that critical new job, or for getting that much longed for promotion. Outside of the career structure, you can devise goals around health and fitness, making new friends, learning new skills and much more. The only limitation is your own creative imagination.

Action Plan	
Goal or Heading:	Start Date:
Your Objective (What you need to do):	Finish Date:
Activity (What are you going to do?):	
Potential Obstacles (What could stop you from doing it?):	
Solutions to Obstacles (What will you do to overcome them?):	
Measures of Success (How will you know when you've met your objective?):	
People to Enlist (Who can help?):	
Review Dates (When will it be reviewed?):	

10

Building Your Brand

"Everything is judged by its appearance; what is unseen counts for nothing. Never let yourself get lost in the crowd, then, or buried in oblivion. Stand out. Be conspicuous, at all cost." – Robert Greene

Branding and Marketing Yourself

No matter what your situation, you should take every opportunity to market and sell yourself. Whether actively looking for a job or not, you should always be conducting a marketing campaign with YOU as the product. The idea of marketing yourself may seem daunting, but it is actually simple and straightforward. It is about connecting with real people and being clear on what you have to offer.

If you are looking for a job or making a career change, taking a proactive approach to actively branding and marketing yourself will put you ahead of the competition. The traditional approach of searching for a job – by signing up with a recruitment agency or responding to job advertisements in the paper – though necessary are available to everyone else looking for a job. This is where you will encounter the most competition and hence lower your chances of being successful. If your sole focus is on this approach you will miss many opportunities in your job search as only about 25 per cent of all jobs are actually advertised, which leaves a sizeable 75 per cent of a hidden job market to tap into. This invisible market is less competitive and therefore the odds of being successful are increased. However, it may take some time for the job offers to materialise through this process, so you will need to have patience.

Below is a four step process to help you get started.

STEP 1 – DEFINE YOUR PERSONAL BRAND

Having a personal brand is about making a statement as to your image, what you stand for and your professional credibility. In marketing terms it is about defining your product offering or USP, unique selling point. Being clear on your personal brand is a way to distinguish yourself from others in your market. Your personal brand is working all the time on your behalf, building your career and reputation.

In addition, developing a keen sense of what you have to offer and creating your own unique selling point focuses your attention on what is important to you and the types of roles you would enjoy. Think about what you are selling. What makes you different or better than other candidates? What are your skills and talents? Is your "product" attractive or do you need to make some improvements (i.e. acquire new skills)? Refer back to your notes from Chapter Five to help you with this exercise.

Once you have pulled this information together you need to summarise it into three personal self-marketing statements: a Career Capsule Profile, a Career Overview Profile and a Key Strengths Profile.

The Career Capsule Profile outlines who you are, what you offer and the potential benefits you bring to the employer. This should be no longer than 30 seconds and should answer the following:

* Who you are

* What you have done

* What you can do

* Brief outline of your strengths.

The Career Overview Profile is an overview of your previous achievements and positions held. It should highlight your most significant achievements and the emphasis should be on your most recent experience. It is not intended as an exhaustive account of your life history and you should be able to communicate this overview in less than five minutes. It answers the question, "tell me about your self".

A Career Overview Profiles should:

* Be interesting, clear and succinct

* Highlight your key achievements and most recent experience

* Focus on the role requirements of the job.

The Key Strengths Profile describes your own unique skills and abilities, the distinguishing features that sets you apart from the other candidates, so it is a very important profile for you to summarise. You should be able to communicate your strengths in two minutes and this profile should:

- Outline your most important skills and abilities
- Highlight what differentiates you from others
- Contain specific examples
- Focus on your achievements.

STEP 2 – DECIDE ON YOUR MARKET

The next step is to decide what market you are in or wish to target, i.e. the type of employer who might be interested in your services. For example, is it a small or large organisation? Operating in the public or private sector? What type of industry is most appropriate (financial, pharmaceutical, services, health, manufacturing, etc.)? Without having a clear picture of the market you are in makes it more difficult to effectively package your service offerings.

You should also consider the needs of any specific organisation you are targeting. For example, is the company introducing a new service or product? Is it downsizing or merging? Are there regulatory issues impacting on it at this time? Being aware of the company's circumstances allows you to fine tune your message to suit its specific requirements.

If you want to gather information about the various companies you might be targeting, begin with the company's website and try to gain access to its annual report. Other resources which might be of help include:

- IDA (www.ida.ie)
- Enterprise Ireland (www.enterprise-ireland.com)
- IBEC (www.ibec.ie)
- Libraries (Ilac Centre or Enterprise Ireland Library)
- Enterprise Area Boards (www.empower.ie)
- Business directories (www.goldenpages.ie; www.kompass.ie; www.whatswhat.ie.)

Finally, you may also want to consider the type of organisation you wish to work for, i.e. the type of culture best suited to your values and needs, the working arrangements which suit your lifestyle, the type of structure and management style that gets the best from out of you and so on. You should have gained some insights on these issues already from the exercises in Chapter Five.

Once you have summarised this information create a marketing statement called a Position or Career Objective Profile which, like the Career Profile, should be something you can say in 30 seconds. Your Position Profile should contain the following information:

- States your preferred work situation or role
- Specifies your targeted industry or market
- Indicates your greatest skills that link to the position
- Defines the level of the position you are seeking.

Finally, one other marketing statement you should consider if you are looking to change jobs is your Exit Statement.

Your Exit Statement expresses positively why you left or wish to leave your job. Without exception, employers will be interested in the reasons why you left or want to leave your job so it is important that you can communicate these reasons as succinctly and clearly as possible, ideally in about 30 seconds.

Your Exit Statement should be:

- Succinct and based on facts
- Free of emotional content
- Presented positively and not critical of anyone.

The preparation of these personal self-marketing statements can give you a real advantage when it comes time to talking about yourself. Once prepared, these statements can be delivered when you need them in any context or situation. Use the table on the following page to write your own statements and be sure to practice them out loud with a trusted friend or colleague so that they become seamless and effortless in the recounting.

Personal Marketing Statements
Capsule Profile (30 Seconds)
Career Overview Profile (3-5 minutes)
Key Strengths Profile (2 Minutes)
Position Profile (30 seconds)
Exit Statement (30 Seconds)

STEP 3 – NETWORKING

Using Effective Networking Channels

Networking is one of the key activities that can get dramatic results whether you wish to advance in your career, find a new job or develop and grow your business. Unfortunately, it can have bad connotations in some people's mind and send others into a state of anxiety. Whatever your feeling on the topic, you really cannot afford not to in engage in this activity. Networking is something we all do on a regular basis without necessarily using that name. It is basically just a fancy term for meeting people, sharing ideas and opening doors so that you can get things done. It is also particularly effective if you are looking to work in a different area or a different industry sector as you can get an insight into what it would be like through talking to others.

In order to gain access to the people who might be interested in your product – YOU – use as many different networking channels as possible, some of which are discussed below.

1. Professional Networking Bodies

Using professional networking bodies is a great way to build up your contacts and to sell yourself and your services. Some of the more common networking bodies are listed below.

Chamber of Commerce

Chambers Ireland is the country's largest business organisation, with 60 member chambers representing over 12,000 businesses throughout the island of Ireland (www.chambers.ie).

Plato

Plato Ireland is a confidential business support forum for owner managers of SMEs (www.plato.ie).

County and City Enterprise Boards

The Enterprise Boards support the start-up and development of local business in Ireland. Supports include advice, mentoring and grants or financial supports for training and growth (www.enterpriseboards.ie).

BNI (Business Network International)

BNI is the largest business networking organisation in the world. It offers members the opportunity to share ideas, contacts and, most importantly, business referrals (www.bni.com).

Rotary International

Rotary club members are part of a diverse group of professionals working to address various community and international service needs (www.rotary.org).

Network Ireland

Provides a forum where women in business, the professions and the arts can exchange ideas and increase their business contacts (www.networkireland.ie).

Women's Executive Network

Offers networking, mentoring and professional development programmes to support and recognise women in managerial and executive positions (www.wxnetwork. com).

2. Social Networking Clubs

One of the easiest ways to gain immediate global presence is through social websites. These social webs are easy to access, logged into by thousands if not millions of members and are usually free of charge. It generally takes no time at all to sign up and get registered. Some of the more popular social webs are listed below.

LinkedIn

LinkedIn is an interconnected network of professionals from around the world, representing 170 industries and 200 countries and with over 36 million members (www.linkedin.com).

Digg

Digg is a social news website for people to discover and share content from anywhere on the Internet by submitting links and stories (www.digg.com).

Facebook

Facebook is a social networking website. Members can join networks organised by city, workplace, school or region to connect and interact with other people (www. facebook.com).

Twitter

Twitter is a service for friends, family, and co-workers to communicate and stay connected through the exchange of quick, frequent answers to one simple question: "What are you doing?" (www.twitter.com).

Second Life

Second Life is a free 3D virtual world where users can socialise, connect and create using voice and text chat. You set up your own business and sell your products and share ideas on-line (www.secondlife.com).

3. Personal Blogs

According to Joseph Jaffe, blogging can actually save your career in these "tumultuous times". Blogging keeps you abreast of what is happening on a global scale and is also a way to establish and promote yourself within a wider community. It has the added advantage of helping to define your talents and interests and it will certainly keep your mind active and sharp. Adam Singer of www.thefuturebuzz.com believes if you aren't blogging you are invisible. He recounts the enormous benefits he has received from blogging, including invitations to speak at different functions, being quoted as an expert source, and reaching a huge audience base.

4. Personal Network Contacts

One aspect of networking that is quick and easy is accessing and using your existing list of network contacts. Brainstorm all the people you know who might be able to help you achieve your goals. Think about relatives, friends, neighbours, colleagues, former colleagues, politicians, college or university lecturers, community or religious leaders, doctors and other professionals and so on. The list is nearly endless so be as creative as possible and don't censor what comes up. You should add to your contact list people you have met through professional networking bodies, social network clubs, conferences, fundraising events, professional societies, parties, courses, voluntary work, etc.

Prioritise Your Network Contacts

Once you have your network contact list drawn up you should prioritise it by creating an Action Priority Matrix to ensure you invest your time wisely. In fact, this matrix can be used for categorising both your career enhancement/job search activities and your networking contacts. It is based on the simple premise that by ordering your wish list into an intelligent pattern you have a better chance of getting the best results and utilising your time and efforts effectively. By not choosing wisely you can get bogged down in low yield, time-consuming activities that prevent you from successfully moving forward.

Breakdown of the Matrix

The combinations for each of the four quadrants breaks down as follows:

- **"Quick Wins"** (High Impact, Low Effort): These are network contacts or activities which are going to give you a high return on your investment with very little effort involved. You should focus on these networks or activities first and make them your priority.
- **"Major Projects"** (High Impact, High Effort): These are network contacts or activities which will take longer to develop or carry out. They will give you a return over the longer term but should be managed carefully so that they don't eat up all of your time and crowd out the quick wins.
- **"Fill Ins"** (Low Impact, Low Effort): These are the network contacts or activities you do if you have the time but should not take up any more of your mental space than is absolutely necessary.
- **"Thankless Tasks"** (Low Impact, High Effort): These are the network contacts or activities that will really eat into your time and will give you very little return. You should avoid these at all costs.

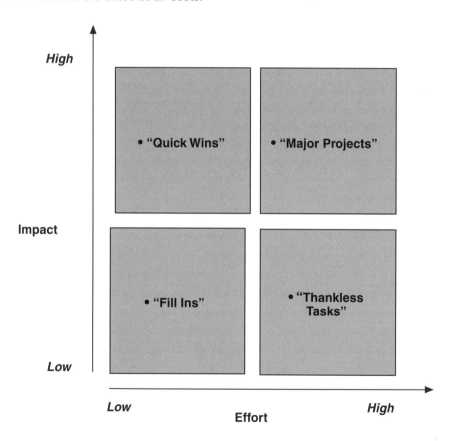

Based on the above matrix, start with your quick wins. Bear in mind when contacting potential employers that the higher up the organisation you can make contact the better. Also, try to speak to the person directly and arrange to meet them face to face. If you can't get together to meet, the alternative in descending order is to telephone, email or write.

Develop Your Network Scripts

Opening Statements at Network Events

When you meet network contacts, either at a function or informally, you will need to work out what you are going to say. Have your Career Capsule Profile, Career Summary Profile, Position Statement and Key Strengths Profile ready. As an introduction to who you are, develop a synopsis of these statements into what is commonly called an "elevator" speech because you will need to be able to deliver it in about 30 seconds, the length of a typical elevator ride. Below is an example of an elevator speech specifically aimed at finding out more information about working in a different industry sector:

> *"Hi, I'm Mary, I'm an engineer working for X company for the last 10 years. I am interested in working in a company that is exploring the development of green energy as I had an opportunity to work on an international project researching this topic last year. I found the developments in this area really exciting and I am looking to develop further the knowledge I have already acquired. I understand you have worked in this area internationally and I would really appreciate if you could give me an insight into what is involved."*

You will probably have a few different elevator stories depending on the background of the people you will be meeting. With any opening gambit or statement, make sure you finish with an invite to the other person to respond using open questions such as the following:

* "Can you tell me more about what is involved?"
* "Do you know anyone who might be able to give me more information?"
* "Are there any openings that you know of in your company or a similar industry?"
* "How can one develop the necessary skills to do that particular line of work?"

Making Contact with Referrals

If you got the name of someone through a contact or through the media, you can either ring and speak to them directly or you can ease gently into it by sending a letter and then following it up with a phone call. Either way, you will need to prepare what you are going to say. Always begin by saying where you got their name from whether it was from the paper or a referral.

Sample opening sentences might include:

"Hi, my name is Mary. We haven't actually had the opportunity to meet, but I was given your name by XY, who suggested I give you a call because they thought you might be able to help me."

Then explain your reason for writing or ringing:

"I am a sales executive working for a company in the financial services area and am currently researching the possibility of moving into the manufacturing sector. I understand from XY that you have considerable knowledge of manufacturing which might be of help to me. I am currently exploring whether I would be suitable for this sector and would welcome twenty minutes of your time to gain a greater understanding of the area."

If you are ringing follow the above by saying:

"Is this something you might be able to help me with and, if so, would it be possible for us to meet perhaps over a coffee at a time that is convenient to you?"

If their time is tight you might want to have an initial chat over the phone, if convenient, and follow up at a later stage with a more detailed discussion, or you could ask them if they know of anyone else who might be able to help. Finish the call by thanking them for their time and confirming the time and date to meet.

If you are writing, close the letter with a follow-up statement about making an appointment and on an optimistic note about being able to help you.

"If this is something you think you could help me with I would really appreciate your time and I will call you next week in the hope that we can arrange a suitable time to meet. Many thanks in advance for your help."

Meeting Referral Contacts

When you meet in person you need to follow up with something more than your elevator speech. You need to explain your reason for wanting a meeting in a lot more detail. Start off by first thanking your network contact for agreeing to meet and then get to the point pretty quickly:

- Summarise what you are looking for – change of career, information on the industry or a new job.

- Explain why you are looking for a new opportunity – have your Exit Statement to hand.

- Give an overview of your Key Skills and Strengths

- Think of a few specific questions you could ask based on your reasons for meeting. For example, "I'm looking for jobs in retail or manufacturing. Do you know anyone that I could talk to?" Or, "You have had a lot of experience in this sector or job. What are the most important skills that one would need to be effective?"

- Avoid making general demands, such as, "Do you know of any jobs that would be good for me?" This sort of question is overwhelming and it puts an undue burden on your contact.

- If appropriate, ask them for names of contacts who might further help you in your search.

- Don't be tempted to overstay your welcome. Finish within the agreed time and thank them again for meeting.

Follow-Up

After you meet with your network contact, be sure to follow up with a thank you note, refer to anything that you found specifically helpful – everyone likes to be appreciated. Be sure to keep in contact so they will remember you if anything comes up, but don't pester them. And, if you make the change or get the job, be sure to let them know. In addition to writing the thank you note you should keep a personal note of the meeting, including what was discussed and any follow-up activities suggested.

11

Promoting and Selling YOU

ANALYSING JOB ADVERTISEMENTS

If you are going down the traditional route of applying for a job that is advertised, you can save time by understanding and responding appropriately to the ads. As a general rule, employers who know what they are doing will have spent considerable time drafting the job advertisement and will have chosen the language they use carefully. There are many clues in the advertisement to help you decide the following:

1. Whether the organisation fits with your values and personal style

2. If you have the necessary qualifications and skills

3. Whether the location, remuneration and benefits are attractive enough for you.

Fully understanding what is in the advertisement can help you prepare your application and also prepare for interview. The basic rule is: only apply for jobs you are suited to and have a good chance of getting. If the advertisement clearly states that a primary degree in business studies is essential and you don't have one, and you have little business experience, then the chances are you won't be shortlisted. However, if you have considerable business experience that you think would really benefit the organisation you might consider placing a call with the contact name on the job advert to check if it would be worth your while applying. Of course, analysing adverts is much easier when you fully know yourself and what you can do, so having completed the other sections in this book will have given you a head start.

Below is a typical job advertisement for a Sales and Marketing Director.

Sales and Marketing Director

Company X is a mid-size financial services firm with a broad range of financial products and services. Founded in 2002, it has been named as one of the fastest growing privately held firms in the United States by INC Magazine and continues to maintain its aggressive pace of growth. It has clients in over 120 countries with operational interests in the US, Asia, Eastern Europe and the Caribbean. With approximately 150 employees the firm has a friendly, close knit start-up environment which is dynamic and hardworking.

We are looking for a hardworking and dynamic Sales and Marketing Director, reporting directly to the CEO, to join our team to help grow a new subsidiary for the firm. Candidates must have experience in the retail financial marketplace.

The Sales and Marketing Director:

- Will be able to demonstrate strong managerial and leadership skills.
- Will have a demonstrable track record selling financial products to retail and institutional clients.
- Can propose a comprehensive marketing scheme and direction of sales growth.
- Can bring new clients and increase revenues from existing accounts.
- Has excellent relationships, with no geographical limitations
- Supports and develops team members.
- Identifies and works collaboratively with key internal customers to understand their needs and to deliver effective and efficient service solutions and improvements.
- Will oversee the development and distribution of communications and promotional materials.
- Coaches and mentors sales staff and others as appropriate.

Sales and Marketing Director

Qualifications

- 5-7 years experience in Promotions, Sales or Marketing
- Business or Marketing Degree
- Excellent negotiation and communication skills
- Should be capable of presenting to internal senior management and external regulatory authorities
- Understanding of the products offered by the business and a familiarity with the processes used to deliver them a plus
- Must be well organised, detail-oriented, efficient and able to work independently and to think critically.

The salary will be commensurate with the position being offered with excellent bonus and benefits package with exciting career prospects in our US division.

Anatomy of a Job Description

Job Title

Job titles are not always a good indicator of what the job entails as different companies may define the role in different ways. Read through the description carefully to find out exactly what is involved. In this job title we know from the description that it is reporting to the CEO so it is the number one Sales and Marketing position in the company. It is also a mid-sized firm which suggests that in terms of positioning in the overall marketplace it may not be as weighty as, say, a Sales & Marketing Director position in a large organisation with 10,000 employees.

Overview of the Company

The company name may or may not be given. Sometimes companies can be advertised by their group name rather than the individual company name. For example, BWG is the group name for Spar and Eurospar. The name also may be that of an agency recruiting on behalf of the organisation.

In the above advertisement the company name has been given so you have the opportunity to do some research on it. Doing your homework on the company is critical at this stage as it will provide you with valuable information that you can include in your letter and CV. If the name of the company hasn't been given you may be able to find it out from the recruitment agency.

You will also get a sense of the culture of the organisation from the overview. In this advertisement you can deduce from the words "friendly", "close knit" and "start-up environment" that it will be quite informal in terms of structure, that working as part of a team will be critical and that individuals will be part of a growing dynamic environment where they will be expected to contribute to the growth of the company. If you are the type of person who likes a culture that is more informal, where guidelines or rules are less rigid, where you are expected to work hard but in a friendly dynamic way and where you have the opportunity to make a real difference, then this culture will appeal to you. When applying you should use similar language in your letter of application and CV. However, if you are the type of person who likes to work with clear structures and rules, where you work more as an individual and less as part of team and where you have plenty of opportunities for promotion and progression then this opportunity may be less appealing.

Overview of the Job Position

The next paragraph usually contains a description of the role that they are recruiting for. It may also include why they need to recruit at this time. They may state where the job is positioned in the company, which in this case is next to the CEO, and the overall purpose of the position, which is to grow a new subsidiary of the business.

In this advertisement they have highlighted a critical component of the job – experience in the retail financial marketplace. They are clearly laying down a marker that they will not select anyone who doesn't have this experience and it will be hard to even get to the next stage unless you have something exceptional to offer. As a rule, if you don't have the required experience, don't apply.

They have also highlighted the words "dynamic" and "hardworking" again so this appears to be an important fit that they will be looking for between the individual and the organisation.

Specific Job Requirements

Most employers have a list of essential and desirable requirements for the role. Outside of the requirement to have financial retail experience, you will also need to have strong management skills so this needs to be included in the CV.

The ability to negotiate and win new clients is another important prerequisite for the role so you will need to highlight where you have done this in previous roles. Provide hard data here in terms of revenue generated and the percentage of key business clients secured.

"Working collaboratively with key internal customers to understand their needs" implies you will need to have strong interpersonal skills, as well as the ability to think more broadly about the future direction of the services provided to meet client needs.

You should be able to meet at least 60-75% of the job requirements to be considered.

Qualifications

You should consider carefully how well you meet the various criteria highlighted in this section. For example, the ad states they are looking for someone with five to seven years' experience, but if you have only three years' experience you should apply anyway as you may be a better fit in other areas. Be honest, but don't be too rigid when it comes to this section.

They have also listed some competencies such as "detail-oriented," "independence" and "critical thinking". As well as demonstrating these in your CV, they are also likely to be assessed at interview.

Remuneration/Career Prospects

Some companies prefer not to mention remuneration at this stage, particularly in Ireland, so you will need to estimate from the advert what a position at that level will typically command. The advert also suggests that they will be looking for someone who is mobile and will see their career prospering in other countries so you will need to check this out in more detail and be clear as to whether or not this appeals to you.

Contact Details and How to Apply

You may be asked to include with your application your remuneration package. If so, don't feel the need to be specific as you can present it in broad terms rather than outlining all of your bonuses and benefits. You may want to suggest that you are flexible around the salary if you feel that your most recent salary was in the higher bracket which could put the employer off.

Whether to Apply for the Job?

Firstly, you will want to consider if the culture appeals to you and whether there is a good fit between your style and their culture. Secondly, you will then want to consider if you have the necessary skills, knowledge and experience to do the job effectively. As already mentioned, if you can fulfil most of the requirements of the role you should apply. You can use the following process to analyse the job advertisement and assess whether you have the necessary skills, knowledge and qualifications for the role.

Step 1

Highlight key words and phrases, such as name of employer, where the job is located, the role requirements and anything about the culture of the organisation, the skills and personal attributes that are required and relevant experience and/or qualifications.

Step 2

Number each word or phrase.

Step 3

Place each word or phrase in a table as illustrated below.

Job Advert Analysis	
1.	2.
3.	4.
5.	6.

Step 4

Think about the words and phrases and what they may mean in this context. What is the employer looking for and how have you demonstrated these requirements?

A sample taking the first paragraph from the job advertisement for Sales and Marketing Director from above is shown on the following page.

Job Advert Analysis	
1. Company X Find out as much as you can about company X. You should include information about their location(s), size, turnover, products and market share, mission, vision, values, and any mergers, acquisitions or subsidiaries they may have.	**2. Mid-size Financial Services** What does this mean in terms of structure and operations? How does it compare to other financial services in the same market?
3. Financial Products and Services What are their main products and services? Which ones are growing and have a competitive edge? Where do you have experience in financial products and services? List those that you know about and research those that you are not so familiar with and may be of interest to the employer.	**4. Founded in 2002** Quite a young company. What is its track record to date? What might a young company like that look like? What is its long-term viability? Will you be comfortable with a financial institute that is fairly new to the market or does that appeal to you?
5. Fastest growing private firm This is a private company which is in a growth phase. This would suggest that it is more likely to have a flatter, leaner structure. Is this something that would appeal to you? It would also suggest that they are looking for someone with drive and ambition as they obviously are ambitious and wish to grow.	**6. INC Magazine** You may want to find out more about INC magazine. Is it respected in this market and what criteria did it use to assess the firm? You may want to note its assessment to discuss at interview.

Job Advert Analysis	
7. Clients in 120 Countries Will this mean that travel is involved and is that something that appeals to you? Also, do you have any languages that might be an asset in dealing with clients from other countries? Or have you had to work with or deal with clients from diverse backgrounds?	**8. 150 Employees** Does the number of employees appeal to you? In a firm like this most of them are likely to be professionally qualified and ambitious. How would you deal with that? Because it is small there will be less of an opportunity to hide, and career advancement opportunities may be limited. However, with an organisation this size the chance to take on different roles may be far greater than in a larger organisation where role demarcation is more pronounced.
9. Friendly and Close Knit Suggestion is that the organisation works very much as part of a team. What team skills do you have that you could address in your CV?	**10. Start-up Environment** Some of the qualities necessary in this type of environment are the ability to be proactive, to take the initiative, to show creativity and to demonstrate resilience. Where have you shown this in the past?
11. Dynamic and Hard Working This is not a place for shrinking violets. What does hard work mean in this context? Is it balanced by the friendly environment? Do you see yourself as dynamic and hard working and where have you shown this in the past?	**12. Other thoughts?**

Once you have analysed the Job Advertisement you will need to be honest with yourself and question whether you have what is required. Then you need to decide whether you really want the job. Are their any gaps and are these significant? Once you have decided you want the job the next step is to write a CV and a covering letter which reflects the fit between what you have to offer and what the employer is looking for.

CREATING A WINNING CV

CV is short for *curriculum vitae* which literally translated means the story of your life. It holds all your hopes and dreams in terms of securing that first job or navigating your way through your career paths. Generally speaking, it is your first introduction to a prospective employer and so it is critically important that you get it right. It has to represent the best you have to offer if you are not to miss out on an attractive opportunity. A CV can be used in the following situations:

1. To apply for a job which has been advertised

2. To canvas potential employers about possible job opportunities

3. To take to recruitment fairs and use in networking opportunities

4. To send to a recruitment agency.

In the current climate employers can receive hundreds of applications for just one job, particularly if the position is advertised through the national press. It is therefore critical that your CV makes an impact and stands out from the rest. You need to think of your CV as a marketing tool, and as such it needs to attract and retain the reader's attention. First impressions matter and if your CV hasn't grabbed the reader's attention in the first 20 or 30 seconds it is unlikely that you will progress to interview. Even more important is the fact that many large organisations use what is called optical recognition technology which scans your CV for the required skills, experience and relevant qualifications needed for the position. Therefore, at a basic level the following principles are important to bear in mind:

1. Keep the layout of your CV as simple as possible. Steer clear of accessorising your CV in any way (i.e. fancy borders, unusual typefaces, graphics) that detracts from the main message you wish to communicate. Occasionally you may want to produce a CV that is radically different from everyone else, i.e. Wanted Posters, but be careful that this type of "off the wall" CV will be well received by the organisation. There are certain industries where this approach might work well, such as advertising, but in most areas it is not a good idea.

2. Keep your CV as concise and short as possible. Employers want to be able to pick out the pertinent information relatively quickly. One page is ideal, two pages more than sufficient. Stand back and think about what it is you wish to communicate. What aspect of your skill set and profile best fit the job position? Use the information from the exercises you completed in this workbook to help you compile your story.

3. You will probably have more than one CV depending on the type of jobs you are applying for. Make sure to tailor your CV to the requirements of the role. Draw attention to the relevant information, i.e. experience and qualifications important to the position, and keep it achievement- and outcome-focused. Use the action words provided on page 194.

4. Keep your language simple and concise. Use words which highlight your key skills, responsibilities and experience and where possible use bullet points rather than writing long sentences that detract from what you wish to communicate. Write it either in the neutral or first person, avoid using the third person.

5. Layout is very important. Don't over-format your CV – no shading or boxes or trying to cram it into one page when it just won't fit. Make sure you can see enough white space. Set margins equally and put section headings in bold type. Make your CV easy to read, in a simple, readable font at a reasonable size and printed on high quality white paper.

6. Check your CV carefully for spelling and grammar and present it flat, not folded. There is no real need to bind or use a cover on your CV as it will only be removed for ease of reading. A staple in the left hand corner of the CV is sufficient.

Types of CVs

There are a variety of different types of CVs which you can use depending on your needs and requirements. The most common types of CVs are described below.

Performance or Chronological CVs

These are the most common type of CVs. Work experience is presented in re-verse chronological order with your most recent work experience captured first. Job titles and company names feature prominently and duties and achievements are described under each job title. These CVs work best when you have relevant experience for the role you are applying for and you want to stay within the same career. They are less effective when you wish to change career or move in a different direction.

Functional or Skills-Based CVs

Functional or skills-based CVs draw more attention to the skills you have developed. These types of CVs are useful when you do not have a lot of experience directly related to the job you are applying for, you are looking to change careers or you have a lot of experience that wouldn't be adequately captured in a chronological CV. For this type of CV it will be important to gather evidence from your life experience (voluntary work, leisure activities and study) to highlight how you have used these skills, and how they link to the position you have applied for. The disadvantage of this

CV is it doesn't demonstrate career growth or promotions and previous employers are not prominent. It is an unusual CV format and not to everyone's taste. Of course, it is possible to use a combination of a skills-based and a chronological CV.

Academic CV

If you are applying for jobs in the academic world greater emphasis will need to be paid to research you have carried out and articles you have published. There will also be more focus on your university qualifications and memberships of any professional bodies, as well as any awards you may have received.

Shorter CV for Part-time Work

This CV needs to be short and to the point – no more than one page – which highlights the key skills and experience necessary to perform in the role effectively.

What to Include in a CV

Regardless of which format you opt for, the following content headings usually form the basis of a good CV:

- **Personal Details**: Include your first name and surname, your address and contact details (phone and email). It is not necessary to put CV at the top of the page as this is taken as a given.

- **Career Summary/Profile**: You should include a three to four line summary of your key selling points related to the job. You should outline your main skills, attributes, knowledge and experience and where they have been gained. This section is optional as it may already be included in your covering letter. The following is an example:

  A Marketing Consultant with over 15 years experience of working with large global organisations in both the public and private sectors. Proven ability to handle complex, resource-intensive multimillion Euro projects. Experienced communicator and team player.

- **Key Skills or Employment History** (Depending on which format you choose or a combination). When outlining your key skills make sure that these are adapted for relevance to the job. If, for example, managing large projects are important you may want to emphasise your project management skills first. As well as highlighting your technical skills, you should also include information on the softer skills you have developed, for example, influencing skills, leadership skills, etc.

Your employment history should begin with your most recent job. Be concise and focus on your skills and achievements rather than tasks. You may want to include more detail on your more recent roles, assuming that there has been a career progression and you have built on previous skills. Don't leave any gaps which may raise questions – if you took a year out mention this in your CV. It is very important that you include the name of the employer, a brief description of their business, employment dates, your job title and where it fits in the reporting line, as well as key responsibilities and achievements.

- **Education**: This should also be listed in reverse order and include the educational qualification gained, the year of graduation and the awarding college. Include any recent study you are undertaking.

- **Professional Development**: Include any training or professional development course you may have undertaken relevant to the job.

- **Other Relevant Information**: This section can include hobbies, interests, membership of any professional bodies or languages spoken other than your native language.

- **References**: Put "References Available on Request" at the end of your CV. It is not necessary to include the names of referees at this point, but you should have alerted the individuals you want references from beforehand to ensure they are happy to do so.

Below are some sample CVs which highlight the different points raised.

A Performance or Chronological CV

Name	Contact Details
Address	Tel (H):
Address	Tel (M):
Address	Email:

PROFILE:

A Marketing Consultant with over 15 years' experience of working with large global organisations in both the public and private sectors. Proven ability to handle complex resource-intensive multimillion Euro projects. Experienced communicator and team player.

KEY SKILLS AND COMPETENCIES:

(these should be reflective of the role you have applied for)

* Significant experience of managing global high profile projects across a range of different industries
* Skilled in dealing with diverse groups at all levels within an organisation
* Strong communication and presentation skills and experience of TV and radio interviews
* Successfully delivered large-scale change projects
* Energetic and collaborative leadership style which fosters development of the team

WORK EXPERIENCE:

Marketing Consultant 2000 – 2009

Oxygen Group is a global marketing and technology organisation which prides itself on its innovation and quality. Listed as one of the top 500 companies in *Fortune* magazine with over 50,000 employees worldwide and with offices in over 49 different countries. Its net revenues for 2008 were €4.5 billion.

JOB RESPONSIBILITIES:

Reporting to the Marketing Director, responsible for the management and operations of large-scale marketing campaigns. This involved managing a budget of €9.5 million and a staff complement of 500. Key responsibilities included:

Management of key resources.....

Liasing with key stakeholders......

Development and design of global campaigns.....

Representing the company at world trade conferences

A Performance or Chronological CV
KEY ACHIEVEMENTS: • Managed a number of successful global marketing campaigns with ….   • Secured new contracts to the value of ……. and doubled our client base to …. in five years   • Successfully managed the merger of x and y   • Developed a new strategic direction for the department and managed to out-source non-productive work activities
EDUCATION: • 2000 – 2002 Trinity College, Dublin. MBA   • 1993 – 1994 University College, Dublin, M.Sc Economics   • 1990 – 1993 University College, Dublin, BSc in Business Studies   • (Leaving Certificate, school and year in same format)
PROFESSIONAL DEVELOPMENT: (Only include if these are relevant to the position)
OTHER RELEVANT INFORMATION: Professional memberships include…..   Received prestigious x award for outstanding contribution in ……   Enjoy sports, travelling, community work…….
REFERENCES: Available on request

Functional or Skills-Based CV	
Name Address Address Address	Contact Details Tel (H): Tel (M): Email:

PROFILE:

An Information Systems and Business Manager with a comprehensive knowledge of financial analysis and business strategy, plus expert skills in IT. Strong analytical and interpersonal skills with a proven track record in delivering on time and within budget.

KEY SKILLS AND COMPETENCIES:

Analytical:

- Analysed different business models and developed a new financial strategy for a multinational organisation.
- Constructed complex statistical models to analyse data using different software packages
- Evaluated, negotiated and planned the roll out of a new IT system for my department

Communication:

- Established and built rapport with various stakeholders, customers and staff
- Presented at various conferences on business systems and models
- Negotiated new service contracts with external suppliers

Teamworking:

- Worked collaboratively with colleagues in evaluating and negotiating the closure of one of our subsidiary offices
- Experience of working in teams during academic projects. This interaction helped develop the ability to work effectively with people from different cultures and work styles
- Represented the company at world trade conferences with other team members

Functional or Skills-Based CV

Creativity and Innovation:

- While at university was responsible for the design, production and delivery of the student newsletter. This involved gathering newsworthy stories, writing and editing material and producing and distributing the final newsletter.
- Designed my own website and blog from scratch, which you can visit at www......
- Wrote articles for newspapers and magazines which have been published in ....

EDUCATION:

- 2007 ongoing: Marketing Diploma in Marketing Institute
- 2000 – 2003: Business Analyst Degree, University of Ulster

PROFESSIONAL DEVELOPMENT:
Have completed a number of graphics and media courses at night

OTHER RELEVANT INFORMATION:
My time away from work is spent cooking, playing videogames and socialising with friends. I play the guitar and regularly play at festivals around the country. I have a strong interest in current affairs and business news.

REFERENCES:
Available on request

Short CV Looking for Part Time Work

Name Address Address Address	Contact Details Tel (H): Tel (M): Email:

CAREER TARGET:

A third year business student with experience in the catering and hotel management sector. Would like to work in a hotel as part of a team within a dynamic and innovative environment.

KEY SKILLS AND COMPETENCIES:

- Excellent interpersonal and communication skills
- Proficient in Microsoft Word, Excel, PowerPoint
- Proven organisational and planning skills to meet tight deadlines
- Self-starter who takes the initiative to make things happen
- Committed to customers and achieving the highest standards of service

EMPLOYMENT HISTORY:

Receptionist – Diamond Hotel, Killarney	Summer & Christmas 2008
Waitress – Chatters Restaurant, Dublin	Summer 2007
Grape Picking – France	Summer 2006

MAIN ACHIEVEMENTS:

- Managed reception and all duties associated with receptionist work
- Liaised regularly with customers to improve the quality of service
- Planned and co-ordinated large functions
- Efficiently resolved enquiries from customers both in person and on the phone
- Developed excellent keyboard and IT skills through data entry using Excel spreadsheets
- Elected as class representative and organised and co-ordinated social and charitable events

Short CV Looking for Part Time Work
QUALIFICATIONS: B.A. Business Studies, X College, Dublin, 2010 Leaving Certificate, X School, 2006
INTERESTS AND HOBBIES: I love travelling and have visited many countries in Europe and Asia. Have a keen interest in sport and play hockey every weekend. Also enjoy films, reading and music.
REFERENCES: Available on request

What Not to Include in Your CV

- Photographs, unless expressly requested by the prospective employer

- Reasons for leaving each job – the place to discuss this is at the interview as writing it down can leave you open to misinterpretation

- Names of referees

- Salary information – this can only be used to reject your application, unless it is specifically requested

- Any sort of failure – exams, businesses, etc.

- List of subjects with grades unless a recent graduate

- Equality legislation does not expect you to include age, date of birth, marital status or religion. Also, leave out weight, height, health or any other personal information that is irrelevant to your application.

- Do not use poor quality photocopies of your CV.

WRITING A COVERING LETTER

A covering letter must be tailor-made to each specific job application. It is the first thing that an employer reads before moving on to your CV, so it is important to make a positive first impression.

Address your letter to the person identified in the job advertisement and state the job you are applying for and where you saw the job advertised (i.e. newspaper, job centre, etc). If your letter is speculative, be specific about the type of job you are looking for.

Clearly outline what you are offering the employer in terms of your skills, knowledge and experience. If the advertisement highlights certain requirements make sure you address these in your letter. As noted earlier, this is your "elevator speech", that 30 second opportunity to sell yourself and make an impression.

Say why you want the job and what attracts you to the company. Make use of the company website, the job advertisement, trade journals, newspapers and other resources to obtain relevant information about the company you are applying to. Relate the letter to the specific needs of the company. This is an opportunity for the employer to see what motivates you about the job and your interest in the company. End on a positive note mentioning your availability for interview and that you look forward to hearing from them.

As with your CV, the letter should be brief, no more than one page. It should be relevant and easy to read, with grammar and spelling carefully checked. Make sure that it is on good quality plain paper.

AIDA Format

Sales and marketers use a format called AIDA to help write their promotional material. You can use this format to help structure your own letter. AIDA stands for Attention, Interest, Desire and Action.

- **Attention** – your letter should contain something that catches the reader's attention and gets straight to the point as to why they should consider your application over others. Your personal marketing statements should be tailored to link in with the specific needs of the role. Pick out key words mentioned in the job advertisement, such as "global", "dynamic", with "business strategic skills", which might be incorporated into your letter as follows: "I have led on many major strategic initiatives with global corporations which combined ingenuity with practical application, working in a dynamic, fast-paced environment."

- **Interest** – outlines your skills, capabilities, knowledge and experience as it relates to the job.

- **Desire** – relates to what attracted you about the role and the organisation and why you want the job.

- **Action** – finish the letter on a positive note about your availability for interview, and that you look forward to hearing from them.

Example of a Covering Letter

Name

Brick Road, Dublin.   Tel: 01-xxx-xxxx   Email: name@gmail.com

Ms. T. White
HR Manager
Global Search
42 Harrow Street
Dublin

28th January 2009

Dear Ms. White,

Re: 24/02 Recruitment Executive Position within a busy HR Department

I would like to apply for the above position as advertised in the Irish Times on Friday the 24th January, 2009 and on your company's website.

As you will see from my enclosed CV, I have recently graduated with a degree in Human Resources from the University of Dublin. I gained a detailed understanding of HR from my degree and a practical knowledge of recruitment and selection through a three month work placement at Recruitment Ireland.

During my placement, I developed a clear understanding of the different aspects of the work of a recruitment specialist, particularly the importance of managing the interface between prospective candidates and employers. I participated in the design of a major recruitment campaign for one of the leading employers in Ireland which gave me invaluable experience in writing and developing job profiles and interview guides, as well as managing and organising my time within a strict deadline.

I have always organised my time effectively, having combined full time academic work to a high standard with part-time paid employment. Whilst working as a receptionist in a busy five star hotel, I built strong customer relationships by assessing clients' needs and deliverying a high quality service.

Throughout my degree, I selected modules that related to HR to prepare myself for a career in this area. I am particularly interested in working for Global Search as I have a keen interest in the recruitment and selection of people working in third world countries following my short stint of working in an orphanage in Romania. I am also very attracted to working for an organisation which has global reach, as I enjoy travelling and visiting other countries and working with people from diverse backgrounds. I believe that my fluency in French and German would be a considerable asset when interacting with people from different countries.

I am available for interview during the month of February and would welcome the opportunity to discuss my application.

I look forward to hearing from you.

Yours sincerely,
Name

Example of a Speculative Letter

You may wish to write to companies which are of interest to you but who have not advertised any job positions. You can use a similar format to the previous covering letter but with a different opening format such as.

I am writing to ask whether you have vacancies within your ... Department.
As you can see from my CV, I have ...

Another approach you can take to finding out about possible vacancies which haven't yet been advertised is to arrange for an informational interview. You could begin your letter by saying:

I am interested in a career in X and would like to know if I could arrange to visit your company to find out more about this type of work and obtain your advice.

I was given your name by Y who suggested that you might be willing to give me some information about careers in this area.

I have recently graduated [or am interested in a change of career] and I have gained valuable qualifications [experience/information/insights] into this area.

I hope you will be able to spare me a half an hour of your time in the near future.

I enclose my CV and will telephone your office next week to try to arrange an appointment at a time that is convenient to you.

Yours sincerely,
Name

Useful Phrases and Vocabulary

Phrases commonly used in describing accomplishments:

Work Achievements

- Improved productivity in _____ by _____
- Successfully convinced [my manager, staff, others etc.] to _____
- Developed [introduced, designed, etc.] a new [program, method, system, etc.] resulting in _____
- Increased staff morale by _____
- Detected a serious error in a [procedure, filing system, ,etc.] and _____
- Improved technological process [service, etc.] by _____
- Successfully arranged and ran a meeting on _____
- Changed _____
- Improved quality control in _____ by _____
- Initiated and implemented a [program, campaign, process, etc.] to _____

Non-Work Achievements

- Created [managed, ran, etc.] a fund-raising campaign for [name of charitable, athletic or artistic activity/group].
- Successfully counselled [advised, helped] a friend.
- Organised [coordinated, etc.] a charitable drive [Neighbourhood Watch Program in my area, etc.].
- Successfully renovated [did the interior design, fixed, etc.] my home myself
- Established [acted as Treasurer, etc.] a professional association [social, athletic club, etc.].
- Acted as a member [or chaired] a committee for _____ .
- Did [oversaw] the decorations for _____
- As a founding member of [name of charity, activity, group], [turned the agency from a low-profile, part-time agency to a high-profile, full-time agency], [created a campaign _____], [successfully raised funds for _____]

Common Action Verbs

achieved	designed	hypothesized	offered	related
adapted	detected	identified	operated	remembered
addressed	determined	illustrated	ordered	repaired
administered	developed	implemented	organized	reported
advised	diagnosed	improved	oversaw	represented
analyzed	directed	improvised	painted	researched
anticipated	discovered	increased	perceived	resolved
arbitrated	dispensed	influenced	performed	responded
arranged	displayed	informed	persuaded	restored
assembled	disproved	initiated	piloted	retrieved
assembled	dissected	innovated	planned	reviewed
assessed	distributed	inspired	played	risked
audited	drafted	instituted	politicked	scheduled
budgeted	dramatized	instructed	predicted	selected
built	drew	integrated	prepared	sensed
calculated	edited	interpreted	prescribed	separated
charted	eliminated	interviewed	presented	served
checked	empathized	invented	problem-	set-up
clarified	energized	inventoried	solved	shaped
classified	enforced	investigated	processed	shared
coached	established	involved	produced	showed
collected	estimated	judged	programmed	sketched
communicated	evaluated	lead	projected	sold
compiled	examined	learned	promoted	solved
completed	expanded	lectured	protected	spoke
composed	experimented	listened	provided	studied
computed	explained	made	publicized	summarized
conducted	enacted	maintained	purchased	supervised
conserved	filed	managed	questioned	supplied
consolidated	financed	manipulated	raised	surveyed
constructed	fixed	mediated	realized	symbolized
consulted	formulated	mentored	reasoned	systematized
controlled	founded	modelled	received	talked
coordinated	gathered	monitored	recommended	taught
counselled	generated	motivated	reconciled	team-built
created	guided	navigated	recruited	tended
decided	handled	negotiated	reduced	tested
defined	headed	observed	referred	transcribed
delegated	helped	obtained	rehabilitated	wrote

THE INTERVIEW

Interviews are still the most widely used method of selecting people for jobs and are set up to provide the employer with the opportunity of meeting you face-to-face and to explore further your suitability for the job. While the employer is making an assessment of your suitability, you also have the opportunity to get to know the organisation better, to meet your future employer/manager and to get a feel for the culture of the organisation. The interview should be a two-way process, so you should do as much homework as you can to ensure that the organisational fit is right for you. There are several different types of interviews:

One-to-One Interviews

These are basically what they appear – a face-to-face interview between you and the employer. These one-to-one interviews can be used as a screening tool to check out your credentials before bringing you to the next stage. If this is the case, it is normally carried out by the HR department.

Panel Interviews

This type of interview is conducted by two or three individuals. Typically, you would have the recruiting manager present, someone from HR and an objective observer. In a panel interview, interviewers agree beforehand on the questions they will ask. There will be a chairperson, who will welcome you and explain the process, the length of time and introduce the panel. Generally, to help you feel more comfortable, the chair will tell you to respond to the person who asked the question rather than having to sweep the panel. If you are not so directed, seek clarification. If nothing else, it will demonstrate your confidence.

Multiple Interviews

Many organisations carry out more than one selection interview. In most situations information in a previous interview is recorded and held for later interviews. You could have up to four interviews which might include initial screening by the HR department or recruitment company (this could also include aptitude tests or personality questionnaires); a panel interview comprised of different members of the organisation including the hiring manager and possibly someone from that team or an internal client who you would be interacting with on a regular basis; interview with the hiring manager's boss; and finally an offer including a discussion on terms and conditions. Each interview generally builds on the previous ones and should gather more specifics on areas that are critical to the role or which have not been fully clarified. Interviewers will also be assessing your fit and suitability with the team and the overall culture of the organisation.

The interview can take different formats depending on the preference of the organisation. The more popular approaches are discussed below.

Competency-based or Behavioural Interviews

A competency-based interview or behavioural interview is a structured interview in which the interviewer's questions are directed at assessing the candidate's qualities and/or capabilities on a number of specific competencies (behavioural areas) important to the role, for example, teamwork, planning and organising or strategic thinking. The basic premise behind this type of interview is that past behaviour is the most accurate predictor of future performance. It focuses on experiences, behaviours, knowledge, skills and abilities that are job-related.

Employment Interviews

Typically, these are unstructured discussions between the interviewer and the individual with no constraints on the types of questions asked. The interview generally revolves around the content of the CV and focuses on general questions such as "Tell me about yourself".

Presentation Interviews

These involve delivering a prepared presentation on a set topic and answering questions on the presentation followed by a standard interview. You would either be sent the topic a few days before the interview to prepare or given some time on the day. You will always be told in advance that you are expected to make a presentation in your letter of invite. Familiarise yourself with the guidelines for the presentation, e.g. the length of time given for the presentation itself and the Q&A afterwards; presentation layout and format; the technology available; and of course the topic to be addressed. If you are using PowerPoint always bring a hard copy of your slides as a back-up and practice your presentation beforehand with a trusted source who will give you honest feedback.

Biographical Interviews

These are semi-structured interviews exploring the individual's past experiences on general topics such as education, work experience, leisure activities and future aspirations. The responses may be rated against each of these topic areas.

Situational Interviews

These are structured systematic approaches to ascertaining the skills and qualities of a candidate. Basically, a predetermined hypothetical question is asked of each individual with each response being scored against a pre-established set of questions.

Assessment Centres

Though not technically interviews *per se,* assessment centres are used by some companies as a way of bringing more objectivity to the selection process. Assessment centres use a multiple assessment approach and have made a major contribution to the selection and development of people at work. They are designed to minimise as many forms of potential assessor bias as possible, and to ensure that each candidate is given equal opportunity to demonstrate their ability across a range of standardised situations. A typical assessment lasts between a half day to a full day and consists of the following:

*   Assessments are made on a number of dimensions considered important for the role, i.e. a set criteria or competency.

*   A variety of assessment techniques are used to increase the reliability of the measurement. The different techniques can include group exercises, presentations, role-plays, aptitude tests, personality questionnaires and interviews.

*   Several assessors or observers are involved in the assessment, again to increase the reliability of what is measured.

*   Generally, several candidates are observed together and rated using a predetermined criterion on their performance.

*   The basic premise of assessment centres is that they reduce selection errors by having multiple exercises, multiple assessors and clearly defined objective performance criteria.

Problems with Typical Interviews

Basically, interviews are inherently flawed and most of those flaws rest with the skill and competence of the interviewer. We have all had the unfortunate experience of a bad interview and unfortunately without proper training in this area the common mistakes that are made will continue. Some of the more common errors are as follows:

*   **Deciding intuitively or using gut-feel**. Studies show that the average time it takes for an interviewer to make a decision on your suitability happens within the first four minutes! And once that decision has been made they spend the rest of the interview confirming their bias.

*   **Placing more weight on negative information than positive**. All relevant studies show that favourable and unfavourable information is weighted differently and that interviewers' impressions more frequently change from favourable to unfavourable than vice versa.

- **Preferring candidates like themselves**. This can be a good thing if you are like them but a very bad thing if you are not!

- **Influencing the candidate's behaviour**. Studies have found that where interviewers had decided to reject candidates, they talked less, and were more critical and formal. This in turn caused the interviewee to feel hesitant and unsure, which affected their responses to the questions.

- **Not allowing adequate time for you to represent yourself** and rushing you through the interview process.

The important point is to **be aware of the frailties of the interview and guard against them**. Remember: the company is also being interviewed and poor interviewers can have an influence as to whether you take the job or not.

Preparing for an Interview

There are a number of key areas which should be covered before the interview.

Your Capability Portfolio

Having completed the exercises in this workbook and your personal self-marketing statements, you are in a good position to plot your skills, achievements, knowledge and capability against the criteria for the role.

Job Requirements and Capability Profile		
Job Requirements	**My Strengths**	**My Weaknesses**
Experience:		
Qualifications:		
Knowledge:		
Skills:		
Other:		

Gather Information about the Organisation

Make sure you have done your homework about the organisation. Use the template below to fill in relevant data about the organisation which you can use as an aide memoir before the interview.

Company Research		
Company Name: **Address:** **Contact Name:**	**Tel No:** **Web Address:** **Contact Number:**	
Number of Employees:	Number of Offices and Locations:	Turnover:
Recent Media Coverage:	Market Area and Segment:	Product Offerings:
Any Mergers/Subsidiaries:	Key Competitors:	Key Strengths:
Key Weaknesses:	Potential Threats:	Any Other Issues:

Gather Information about the Interviewers

Find out as much as you can about who is going to be interviewing you – their background, job title and what department they are in. If at all possible, find out about their style and approach, how they typically act (are they brusque or easy-going) and what is high on their agenda (cost cutting, market growth, people issues, etc.)

Prepare Responses to Questions

Having carefully distilled what is required for the role you should prepare your answers to possible questions that might be asked. You should identify situations where you have demonstrated the key knowledge, skills or behaviours that the organisation is looking for. During the interview your responses should be specific and give enough detail to demonstrate your competence in the area. This is particularly true where an interviewer uses a competency or behavioural interview approach. Tell them about a specific situations that relates to what they looking for, not a general one. Briefly tell them about the situation, what actions you took, and the positive result or outcome. Your answer should follow the STAR method (Situation, Task, Action, Result).

Star Method

- **S**ituation: Describe situations that demonstrate your strengths and have a positive outcome
- **T**ask: Outline what was involved
- **A**ction: Discuss the various actions you took
- **R**esult: Describe the results of those actions and their benefits.

Before the interview, pick two or three key areas that reflect your capabilities and that you wish to discuss at interview using the STAR method. Make sure you practice your response so that they flow easily during the interview process. Typically, the interviewer will pick your responses apart with key questions, so be prepared to answer such questions. Where possible, quantify your responses as this lends more weight to your responses. For example, if you managed a team, mention the number you managed, what your budget allocation was (if any) and the sales or production figures you reached.

Be prepared to discuss when results didn't go as well as planned and what you learnt from this and how you ensured that those poor results didn't happen again. A sample STAR process is outlined below.

- **Situation**: "I took responsibility for the management of our training department, which provides in-house training to our internal customers. I was responsible for 12 staff and a budget of 1.5 million euro."
- **Task**: "I noticed from our evaluation sheets that over 40 per cent of our clients were dissatisfied with the quality of our ECDL courses and from our database that attendance at these courses had dropped by 30 per cent over the past three years. I wanted to do something to improve these numbers."
- **Action**: "First, I organised the team to contact our existing customers and get feedback on our overall service, and in particular on the dissatisfaction ratings on our ECDL course. We then redesigned the programme based on the feedback and trailed it with one of our subsidiary groups. We next ran a promo-

tional campaign highlighting our 'new and improved' course with an offer of a free place on any of our other courses for the first 20 people who signed up."

- **Result**: "We came up with a very successful EDCL course, utilised some great ideas to improve other aspects of our service, and raised the satisfaction ratings up to 90 per cent and raised attendance by 18 per cent the first year."

During the Interview

Types of Interview Questions

There are many different types of questions which can be asked at interview, and this section by no means captures all of them, but it will give you a guideline as to the questions which you may be asked and give you an opportunity to prepare.

Types of Interview Questions	
Type of Question	**Possible Responses**
"Tell me a little about yourself."	• This is one of the opening questions favoured by a lot of interviewers. It is often used to help you ease into the interview. • It is critical that you are specific and you can summarise succinctly the relevant points about yourself. Your Career Capsule Profile is what you should use at this point as it ensures you can provide the highlights in two to three minutes. • Talk about your most recent career experiences and highlight anything of particular relevance from the past (awards or major achievements).

Types of Interview Questions	
"What unique qualities or attributes would you bring to the job?"	• This is a very open-ended question and one where you can get caught waffling – your Key Strengths Profile should come in handy at this point. Again, you should be able to summarise your qualities or attributes in three to five minutes. • Make sure you link your unique qualities to the role you have applied for and highlight these specifically.
"Why did you leave your last job?"	• State your reasons for leaving clearly and factually. • If there were negative reasons for leaving, stay factual and don't use emotive words. • Have your Exit Statement ready so you don't find yourself over-compensating in your answer. • Try where possible to express positive reasons and answers when answering this question. Never blame anyone or anything else. • "I was ready for a greater challenge", or "Each job offered a better opportunity, which I took" are appropriate responses.

Types of Interview Questions	
"What has been your biggest disappointment in your career to date?"	• Like the question on strengths and weaknesses, this can give an interviewer a clue into how insightful you are about yourself. • It can also point to specific requirements you have for a role so be careful that you don't say things that run counter to what the job provides. • It can also tell an interviewer how good you are.
"What would you bring to the company if we employed you?"	• This is an opportunity to sell yourself and to highlight the strengths of the role and how they match with your own skill sets, knowledge and experience. • It is also an opportunity to capture aspects of your talents that may not be coming through readily in the other types of questions which are asked.
"What did you achieve in your last job?" **Or,** **"What have been your greatest achievements?"**	• Prepare a number of relevant examples and explain one using the STAR method. • Be sure that you are the one who features as the one who made a difference. • Your examples should clearly highlight any benefits to the organisation, such as increased profits, cost saving, quality improvements, winning new contracts, etc.

Types of Interview Questions	
"Why do you want to work here?"	• This is an opportunity to say what you know about the company and to highlight any research you have done about its future direction, its mission, values and vision statement and about the culture. • An employer will be keen to hear about your interest in the organisation.
"What would you hope to achieve in your first 12 months in the job?"	• This is where your research about the company and the role will be critical. You will need to identify key issues that the organisation would like to address and explain how you would deal with them. • You should also do some high level strategic planning about how you see the role developing. Think about how the role could evolve and grow; how it could be structured; what systems and processes would be in place; what the culture and relationships would be like. • Emphasise your personal strengths that are relevant to the role requirements.

Types of Interview Questions	
"What are your strengths and weaknesses?"	• A firm favourite with interviewers and one given the current climate around Emotional Intelligence can tell them a lot about how you view your own development and how insightful you are about yourself and hence others. • It's easy for most people to rattle off their answers about their strengths but many find it more difficult to discuss their weaknesses – and wonder whether they should say anything about them. • Different experts in the field have different views on what you should say about your weaknesses. Some say you should fudge the issue and give the standard pat answers such as "I get inpatient with sloppy work", or "I am a perfectionist". However, others believe that insights into your weaknesses, learning from them and moving on can have beneficial effects for both the person and the organisation and that lack of self-awareness can lead to derailment in a career. An experienced interviewer will use this knowledge wisely so you will need to make a judgement call as to how you choose to respond to this question.

Types of Interview Questions	
	• At the same time, be astute in your answers – saying, for example, you are a compulsive liar will pose more questions than it does answers.
	• Position your weaknesses as growth opportunities and give examples of the things you have done to overcome them.
	• Again, like everything, try out your answers on a trusted advisor.

COMPETENCY-BASED OR BEHAVIOURAL INTERVIEWS

These are very effective techniques as they get you to recount how you have demonstrated the behaviour, skill and/or knowledge in different situations in the past. They are based on the premise that past behaviour is a good predictor of future behaviour. Interviewers favour this approach as it has a clear structure, answers are evaluated and rated against pre-determined criteria and candidates can be compared across the different competencies.

Questions usually focus on eliciting specific examples from an interviewee, describing situations where they might (or might not) have demonstrated the required behaviours. These are then probed in a systematic way by the interviewer to build up a picture of the relative strengths and weaknesses of the individual on that competency. The process generally follows the guidelines below. The competency area and definition are outlined first:

"The area we want to look at is teamwork. We are particularly interested in how well you have worked as part of a team in the past and how you have dealt with competing agendas within the team."

Followed by an open question:

"What opportunity have you had to work as part of a team"

Or

"When have you worked as part of a team where there was conflict and you helped to resolve it"?

206

In this instance the interviewer is looking for a specific example from your past experience either in work, school, college or leisure activities.

Having opened it up, the interviewer will then proceed with probing questions along the following lines:

"What skills do you bring to a team?" (behavioural examples)

"On reflection what could you have improved upon?" (learning)

"What feedback did you get about how well you performed?" (appraised by others)

"How do you think your teamworking skills compare to others?" (comparative)

"Now you've had experience of working in that way, what advice would you give to others?" (knowledge of best practice)

Typically, a 45 minute interview would cover six competency areas with appropriately six minutes given over to each area, which allows time at the beginning for introductions and for any questions you may have at the end. A sample of the types of areas covered and questions asked are outlined below.

Planning and Organising

"How do you typically go about organising your work?" (What approaches do you take to help you stay organised? How do you compare with others who you regard as being very organised? When have you missed a deadline?)

"We all have projects which do not go exactly as we planned. Tell me about a project you managed which did not go as you expected." (What went wrong? What did you do to rectify the situation? What did you learn and how would you approach the task differently the next time around?)

Decision Making

"Give me a time when you have had to stand by a controversial decision that you have made?" (How did you feel about this? What exactly did you do? How successful were you?)

"Give me an example of a time when your decision making was ineffective." (What went wrong? What would you do differently?)

Technical Skills

"How have you gone about keeping up-to-date within your area of specialism?" (What interest do you take in new developments happening within your area? How do you go about staying abreast of what is happening?)

"What do you most enjoy about the technical aspects of your job?" (Why is that the case? How do you manage the least enjoyable aspects?)

Teamwork

"When have you had to work with others to solve a difficult problem?" (How did you work with other people in the group? What tensions or difficulties arose? What did you do to ensure that the best solution was chosen?)

"Tell me about a particularly effective team you have worked in?" (What made it effective? What was your role? What contribution did you make to the team?)

Leadership

"How do you ensure that your team is focused on achieving the organisation's strategic objectives?" (Describe the process? What were the results? How do they compare with other teams?)

"Give me an example of a time when you experienced difficulty/problems in getting the team to accept your leadership." (What did you do to over come this? How were you sure that you had successfully overcome the difficulties?)

"What opportunities have you had to take the lead in a team?" (What was the situation and how did it arise? How did you ensure the team achieved the result it was looking for?)

Influencing and Persuasion

"Who have been some of the toughest groups of people you needed to win around to your way of thinking?" (Why were they difficult? How did you go about influencing them? How successful were you?)

"Can you tell me about a time when you have had to influence someone outside of your team in order to achieve your objectives?" (How did you go about it? How did you adapt your approach? How successful were you?)

Building Relationships

"How do go about establishing rapport and building relationships with people you don't know well." (Give me an example of when you had to do this. What was the outcome?)

"With which kinds of people have you found it difficult to develop relationships?" (Can you tell me why? Can you give me an example?)

"When have you been reluctant to challenge someone's views?" (Why? Are there particular situations or people who challenge you more than others?)

Resilience

"When have you faced major setbacks in your work?" (How did you deal with them?)

"When have you been faced with a particularly difficult challenge?" (How did you motivate yourself? What setbacks did you need to manage?)

"What have been some of your biggest disappointments in your career to date?" (How have you dealt with them?)

Initiative

"What extra responsibilities have you taken on in the last eighteen months?" (What extra pressure has this put upon you? How did you cope with it?)

"What is your major source of satisfaction in your job?"

"What steps have you taken to develop your knowledge and skills of the role?" (What further plans do you have for self-development?)

Customer Service

"What standards do you aim to achieve in your work, and how do you measure these standards?" (When did you feel that you fell short of your current standards? Why was that?)

"How do you maintain a good quality service to your customers?" (What sort of activities have you undertaken to maintain and improve on the quality of service?)

"When have you had to handle a difficult customer in the past?" (Why was the customer difficult? What steps did you take to resolve the situation? What was the outcome?)

QUESTIONS TO ASK THE INTERVIEWER

At the end of every interview there should be an opportunity for you to ask questions. Make sure you grab this with both hands — it is expected. Asking good well researched questions provides you with the opportunity to demonstrate your understanding of the issues facing the organisation and can help you to stand out from the rest of the candidates who have applied.

It is also your opportunity to take control of the interview and raise any issues you would like to discuss or to put forward any aspects of yourself that might be missed by the interviewer. This is an opportunity to impress the interviewer so avoid the impulse to ask the more mundane questions or the belief that you will think of something great at the time – you won't! Do your homework beforehand and it will pay off. The questions you ask should centre on the job priorities and how to make a difference to the performance of the organisation. Put your CEO or consultant hat on and try to think strategically about the organisation and what the CEO or senior management might be grappling with. You want to get that *WOW* factor going in the interviewer's mind by asking questions that challenge their own thinking or which demonstrate that you have really thought about the organisation. The following are a list of questions you could ask, and following that is a list of definite "no-no" questions.

Good Questions to Ask

"How might this role positively impact on the overall performance of the business?"

"What are the critical things I need to be doing from your perspective in order to make an impact in the first 100 days?"

"I notice that you have just come through a major restructuring of your business. Are you exploring other product offerings within the marketplace and, if so, how do you think this role could contribute to the development of these products?"

"If someone were to come into this role and begin to make a significant impact on the organisation, what sort of changes would you want to see happening, and how would this be measured?"

"How would you describe the culture of the organisation and what are your most important values?"

"I am aware that you operate in a very fast-paced environment. How does this impact on your strategic planning?"

"How do you think this role might develop and progress in the future?"

"I have read that you are ... (this is good sentence to start with and can be anything to do with proposed mergers, cost cutting, operating profits, business expansion or competitors in the marketplace). How do you think this role might support you in this regard?"

Definite "No-No" Questions

"How many weeks' holidays do I get?"

"What are the start and finish times?"

"Do I get a car and what are the benefits?"

"What are the pension arrangements?"

"Will I be guaranteed a job a year from now?"

"What size is my office?"

After the Interview

This is an opportunity for you to note your performance, what went well and what didn't go so well, so that you can build and improve. Going for interviews is a skill and if you haven't done it for a while you may be out of practice so try to learn from each one.

12

Creating the Mindset for Success

"It is never too late to be what we might have been." – George Eliot

FUTURE PROOFING YOUR CAREER

Given the current downturn in the global economy, you might be wondering what you need to do to future proof your career and ensure you remain employable now and in the future. Some of the things you might consider are described below.

Think Creatively

You need to think outside the box about the types of roles you might be suited for and the type of work you would like to do. As already discussed, career ladders are becoming a thing of the past. Challenge yourself about what type of role will be most satisfying and fulfilling for you. Are their gaps in your competence level that could be fulfilled by taking a lateral move, or maybe even a backwards move? If you have strong relationship skills and work in accounting is now the time to move into sales or customer service? Maybe it is time to take a career break, if you can afford it, and consider working overseas or taking up voluntary work. Do you have specialist skills or an idea that would allow you to start up your own business? The important point to keep upper most in your mind is that you are now in charge of your career and you need to think like the CEO of YOU.

Be Flexible

You need to be open and flexible to the types of work contracts that are on offer. As companies look to rationalise their services they have to come up with more creative ways of staying competitive, whilst at the same time ensuring they have the needed resources to deliver their services. There are a number of approaches companies are taking including:

- Extended career breaks – though you are off the payroll you still have the option to return to your employment with the company once business picks up again.

- Reduced working week – some companies are reducing the hours people work from a full five day week to a four or three day week.

- Contract or project work – you can get this type of work through the traditional routes of job advertisements, direct marketing of your services or through interim solution companies. Interim solutions are a way of filling critical gaps in company's resources for an agreed period of time. It may be to cover maternity leave, fill an important position in a project group, help in a crisis situation, or help implement changing work practices. Interim solutions are hassle-free from a company's point of you as the screening, recruitment and payroll are all covered by the interim company. If you have a lot of experience in a particular area this may be an option you might consider exploring.

Develop Your Skills and Knowledge Portfolio

You should be constantly updating and developing your skills. Now might be a good time to consider further education to build your qualifications. Look for work that stretches your portfolio of skills and builds your knowledge and competency levels. Elect to take on extra work or get involved in projects that you are unfamiliar with. Not only will you enhance your skills but it is a great way of building your profile in an organisation. With technical skills changing so rapidly you should think about developing your non-technical skills such as influencing, planning or team management. If you are finding there is less of a demand for your particular technical skill set think about developing skills that are becoming more popular. At the same time, think about the skills you have developed such as negotiating, training, detailed planning, time management, etc. and how they might be adapted and used in another line of work. This may also be a good time to learn a new language as the global market opens up.

Think Globally

Continue to build your knowledge and understanding of business trends, your profession and the economy by reading business journals, newspapers and surfing the web. If you get an opportunity to work abroad this will greatly enhance your skills and knowledge as it will expose you to different cultures and to working with diverse groups. You will also gain a greater appreciation of how businesses work in a global context.

Build Your Profile

Networking is a critical practice to engage in whatever your circumstances. It is important to build a set of contacts who can help you with potential opportunities or jobs. Chapter 10 on Building Your Brand has some excellent ideas on networking.

Stay Positive

This will not only be advantageous to you and your health but is an attractive attribute to others. People usually prefer to work with people who are agreeable and positive. Apply the five principles for "Staying on Track" in this chapter. If you are currently out of work and searching for a job look for ways to keep yourself occupied by helping out friends or neighbours or by working in the community. Stay engaged by doing voluntary work and keep to a regular schedule during the week as if you were actually in paid employment. Think of the current downturn as an opportunity for you to do things you have always wanted to do and to explore different career opportunities. When our backs are against the wall we tend to be at our most creative, so let those creative juices flow.

Know YOU

Stay up-to-date on what you have to offer. Develop a clear picture of your knowledge, skills and interests. Complete this workbook faithfully and have your CV ready just in case.

STAYING ON TRACK

It can be all to difficult to keep going, even with the best will in the world and all the right tools at our disposal. Most of us start out with great intentions only to find our enthusiasm begin to wane half way through, particularly when the results aren't coming in the way we would like. This is called the "Dark Night of the Innovator" and typically describes the dip in enthusiasm or energy we all experience when undertaking a new project or task. We can also allow the fear of what might or might not happen strangle and rob us of our motivation and our energy. So how can you ensure that you succeed in whatever you have set your sights on? There is no magic formula, but below are five suggestions which, if you follow them through, will ensure you a greater chance of success.

1. Learned Optimism

Thomas Edison made hundreds of attempts at the light bulb before he found success. When asked why he kept persevering, he replied, "For each attempt that failed and was discarded, it put me one step closer to the one experiment that would succeed." For each thought, each belief that created a reality that wasn't quite right, a new thought took its place, creating a better reality.

Edison appreciated the fact that we get very little say over what happens to us but we get 100 per cent say over how we respond to these things. Our inner dialogue can empower or limit us. We need to be particularly vigilant about those little voices that seem to distract, and put doubt and fear in our minds, eroding our vision and confidence and telling us it's no use, it will all end up in disappointment. But if we give up at the first sign of disappointment then we will likely consign ourselves to the "what could have been" brigade.

Watching your self-talk is critical to maintaining motivation and energy to accomplish your goals. As Mahatma Gandhi said, "a man is but the product of his thoughts. What he thinks, he becomes". But watching our self-talk alone is not sufficient to ensure success and happiness. Managing our thought patterns is also important.

One of the leading experts on thought patterns, Dr. Martin Seligman, looked in particular at the impact of an optimistic versus a pessimistic outlook on life and success. So what separates optimistic people from more pessimistic people? Seligman says it's the way we explain events and outcomes to ourselves. If something good happens to us, how do we explain it? Was it luck? Or was it the result of our talent? If something bad happens to us, how do we explain that? Is it that conditions just weren't right? Or did the bad event happen because we're somehow flawed as individuals? Will this flaw impact on all our endeavours?

After extensive research, Seligman concluded that optimists and pessimists attribute the reasons for success and failure differently. Pessimists tend to believe bad events are their fault, that the effects will last a long time and will undermine everything they do. Optimists see failure as a setback, not their fault, with short-term effects and are confined to this one event. Seligman's concepts are explained more fully in the table on the following page.

There are good reasons for being optimistic. For example, optimists have fewer problems with infectious diseases and have healthier immune systems; sales people with optimistic styles had 88 per cent more success than pessimists; and Seligman was able to predict election winners by analysing their speeches for optimistic content!

Seligman points out that optimism is essential to success in many careers and that a lack of optimism limits one's life. However, there is a cautionary warning to optimism. Seligman says a pilot, for example, shouldn't be "optimistic" the wings of his plane won't ice up and fail to de-ice them before a flight. Pessimism can sometimes be useful because it forces us to confront situations where we are not in control and must change course. (Relentlessly optimistic people seem to be somewhat blinded to reality.)

	Optimists	Pessimists
Permanence	Confident that you will get things back on track quickly. "I lost my job. Thank goodness there are other opportunities available."	Bad times or events will carry on forever. "I lost my job. I'll never find one as good again, no point even trying."
Pervasiveness	Bad events are specific to this situation. "I lost my job. Thankfully I have my health and my family and good friends."	Bad events undermine everything I do. "I lost my job. And I just know that everything else is going to go wrong."
Personalisation	Bad events are brought on by bad luck or other people. "I lost my job. Obviously my skill set isn't needed at this time."	Bad events are the result of my influence. "I lost my job. If only I had tried harder or been a better employee this wouldn't have happened."

So how can we improve our optimism? Seligman offers a solution called the ABCDE approach, which is based on the pioneering work of Albert Ellis who developed Cognitive Behavioural Therapy (CBT).

- A relates to the adverse or activating event.
- B relates to the beliefs that we hold about that event
- C relates to the consequences of those beliefs
- D relates to disputing or challenging those beliefs, where we find evidence against the negative beliefs, alternatives to our negative reasoning, and limit the implication of the beliefs. Seligman writes: "Much of the skill of dealing with set-backs ... consists of learning how to dispute your own first thoughts in reaction to a setback."
- E is for energisation, which we feel after we've disputed our false, negative beliefs.

One simple way of changing negative self-belief is through a process known as re-framing. In the development section on positive attitude we showed that we have a higher percentage of negative self-talk than positive self-talk so it is important that we have a mechanism to counteract it. Reframing is a technique that can be used to replace negative self-talk with positive self-talk. The table below shows how common negative self-statements can be changes into positive ones.

Changing Negative Thoughts/Statements into Positive Ones	
"I don't deserve this job."	"I belong here and I am good at my job."
"I don't want to let my team down."	"I believe in myself and my team believes in me."
"I don't want other people to think badly of me or talk behind my back."	"What other people think is their own responsibility."
"I am embarrassed when I make mistakes."	"It's ok to make mistakes; I will learn from them."

By consciously trying to change our negative thought patterns we redirect the focus of our attention to initiate self-encouragement and motivation. By trying to reframe our negative beliefs into positive ones we are helping to reshape destructive reasoning or self-beliefs. Reframing can help us to indentify and modify our perceptions to get a new meaning of the problem.

Activity

What are your most persistent negative thoughts? Record them on the table on the following page. Do they follow the permanence, pervasiveness or personalisation pattern? How can you rewrite these to be more positive?

Change Destructive Self-Statements into Constructive Ones	
Negative Self-Statements	**Positive Self-Statements**

2. Self-belief or Self-efficacy

Self-belief or self-efficacy is believing that you can solve most problems that you encounter and that you have faith in your ability to succeed. It means not allowing doubts to creep in and undermine you, and it shows others that you are confident and believe in yourself. Unlike Learned Optimism, which is about managing your self-talk, self-belief or self-efficacy is about taking control and stating what it is you want to achieve on a regular basis, rather than leaving it to chance. You can do this by creating and repeating your own affirmations. Below is advice on how to write affirmations. The more you adhere to these principles, the more effective your affirmations will be.

Writing Affirmations

Focus on what you want, not on what you don't want. For example, if you want to stop eating chocolate or stop smoking, don't say, "I want to stop eating chocolate or stop smoking" because that focuses the mind on the behaviour you're trying to stop. If you keep thinking about eating chocolate or smoking, you'll feel like eating chocolate or smoking! Instead, focus on what you want by saying, "I want to live a healthy lifestyle". Your subconscious is now programmed to focus on a healthy lifestyle and it knows that to achieve one it is necessary to cut out anything that will prevent it, like eating chocolate or smoking. It will, therefore, create a desire in you to quit those habits.

Use the present tense. Don't say, "I *will* grow confident", otherwise your sub-conscious will keep postponing your desire to "some day" in the future. Instead say, "I *am* growing confident".

Keep your affirmation as brief as possible. Focus on one or two issues at a time. Once your affirmations begins to materialise (typically, in a few weeks), you can move on to another issue or two with a new affirmation.

Be as specific as possible. For example, instead of saying, "I am growing more confident", say in what ways, such as, "dealing with people" or "giving presentations" and put a timescale on it.

Practicing Your Affirmations

There are many ways to practice your affirmations. You can repeat them to yourself when you are exercising or going for a walk. Or, another really powerful way to embed them in your subconscious is to write out your affirmations before you go to sleep and allow them to percolate through your subconscious mind while you are sleeping. You can also repeat them at the end of a relaxation or meditative exercise or write them down and place them in key places in your home or office. Whatever method you choose, the most important point is that you repeat them religiously to yourself every day. Keep a journal and record all the changes that are occurring because of your affirmations. This will keep you focused, strengthening and speeding up the results. Persistence and repetition are the keys. Energise your affirmation with emotion. How will you feel after you achieve the desired results? Experience those feelings now by visualising your success. This will energise your affirmation and help it to bear fruit.

Manifesting Your Affirmations

Don't just sit back, waiting for your affirmation to magically transform your life. Start making things happen today. Your actions and affirmations support and reinforce each other. When affirmations and action steps are practiced simultaneously, explosive power is released and your success is assured. So do both.

Reinforcing Your Affirmations

The procedures outlined above are sufficient to start reprogramming your mind. However, to hasten and strengthen your results, you can reinforce your affirmations by getting CDs which focus specially on refocusing the mind in certain areas. Pick one which applies to you.

3. Impulse Control

Impulse Control or deferred gratification is about putting off your impulses for instant gratification until you can truly manifest your desires. This ability to delay gratification is considered to be a personality trait and is thought to be important for life success and, according to Daniel Goleman, people who possess emotional intelligence score highly on impulse control. Deferring gratification means saying no to things that we think will satisfy us, knowing that it will be a short-term gain and may even move us further from our goal.

There is a clear correlation between the time and effort someone puts in and the success they ultimately achieve, whether it's related to losing weight, becoming fitter or learning a new skill. According to Malcolm Gladwell in his book *Outliers*, nearly without exception those who we deem to be "socially successful" have put in the necessary hours (10,000 hours is the minimum practice time needed to achieve world class performance) to excel in their chosen field and are not just the product of "lucky genes".

One of the more notable examples he cited was Bill Gates. Before Bill Gates dropped out of Harvard and set up Microsoft he had averaged 10,000 hours on software programming. It's true to say that Gates had other advantages in that he had a natural talent for computers and was in a position both economically and socially to work with them at a time when it was far from common place. Leaving those factors aside, he still put in an inordinate amount of time to perfect his skills, including getting up at 3.00 am when there was limited access to the computer. You could say that as an adolescent Bill Gates knew what impulse control was all about. While his friends were off partying and playing sports, Gates was perfecting his skills and preparing himself for the future and, as they say, the rest is history.

But in order to be able to dedicate the needed time and effort there are two other critical points which come into play. Firstly, you must do what is important and meaningful to you. Hopefully, at this stage in the workbook you will have found out what that is and you are working towards creating the life and career of your dreams. And secondly, there is a link between reward and effort. When you track your successes and you begin to see the link between the sacrifices and the effort you are putting in, you are more likely to stay the course.

It's like losing weight. When you get on the scales and see the pounds dropping off it makes the sacrifices that much easier to endure and spurs you on until you have reached your goal. So take the opportunity now to briefly record your key goals below and track on a daily basis the actions you have taken that are moving you closer to them. At the end of each week, make a note of the progress you have made and take time to celebrate your success. Use the sample template below to develop your own goal progress tracker.

Goal Progress Tracker

Key Goals	Mon	Tues	Wed	Thur	Fri	Sat	Sun
1.							
2.							
3.							
4.							
5.							
6.							
7.							
Progress Made:							

4. Emotional Regulation

Obstacles and challenges are a normal part of everyday life. They teach us something about ourselves that is important to our self-development as human beings. They oftentimes equip us with extraordinary skills and qualities not easily achieved when times are easy. However, there are periods when it appears everything is a struggle and nothing seems to be going right, and it is at these times that our emotions can take control of our logical mind, leaving us at times feeling out of control. Emotions are our internal barometers warning us that there is something we need to pay attention to.

Emotional regulation is not about denying or repressing your feelings. Emotions such as anger, sadness and fear can drive us to being very productive and creative. Emotional regulation is not about over-control of your emotions. In fact, stifling your emotions and repressing them can lead to illness. Being able to identify the emotion and recognise why it arose is an important first step. The next step is to manage the emotion appropriately so that is serves us rather than the other way around.

The following steps to dealing with your emotions will help you manage them more effectively:

1. Become mindful of your current emotions
2. Change emotions by doing the opposite action
3. Become aware of critical times.

Become Mindful of Your Current Emotions

Meet your emotions simply and directly without trying to repress or exaggerate them, allowing your body to go through its various physiological processes for dealing with them. Simply observe your emotions and experience them as a wave coming and going. Try not to block, suppress or get rid of the emotion, instead simply experience it. When we try to block or suppress our emotions we often find that we end up exaggerating our emotional experience. If you view emotions as energy passing through you, you will appreciate the need to let that energy flow. If it gets blocked or trapped, it is like a pressure cooker that builds up a head of steam and what initially might have seemed like a mild reaction becomes quite extreme. Just as energy has a finite life, so too have emotions and they will eventually dissipate. It's important not to hold on to emotions or amplify them in any way. Remember, you are not your emotion and you do not have to act on them.

Change Emotions by Doing the Opposite Action

If you feel angry avoid what is making you angry rather than attacking it. Do something nice rather than mean. If the emotion is fear, which urges us to run away, the opposite action teaches us to face what we fear over and over until we become confident that we can deal with it. Depression pushes us to hide away and give up so the opposite action is to engage in activities and meet people until we feel better. It can sometimes help when in the grip of an emotional experience to visualise yourself floating out of your body and looking down at yourself in the current state. As an observer, you can then look more dispassionately at the situation and think about it in a more logical way. In this position, if it is anger you are feeling you can imagine sympathy and empathy flowing into you and to the other person or situation which has caused the anger.

Distract yourself by doing something that takes your mind off the situation or hurtful comments. Get involved in some form of exercise or a hobby. Generate opposite emotions such as watching comedies on TV, or reading humorous books. Do something that requires mental concentration like counting backwards by sevens from 100. In any of these activities, the important thing is to really focus on what you are doing. If you continue to ruminate about the problem or the hurt feelings while doing any of these techniques you will experience less benefit. Pick something you can get into, pay attention to the details of it, and bring your focus back if your mind wanders.

Become Aware of Critical Times

Become aware of the times when you are most vulnerable, such as being tired, pre-menstrual, hungry or sick. These will strongly affect your emotional experience so at these times avoid situations which will increase your stress levels and cause emotional outbursts. Do something pleasant for yourself like soaking in the bathtub, going to the cinema in the middle of the week, visiting an art gallery or museum, buying your favourite magazine or newspaper and finding a quiet place to read it while you drink a cappuccino, or eat a muffin or both! Whatever your favourite activity is, find it and do it at these times.

5. Reaching Out

Finally, take risks and make an effort to get involved in new and different situations and with new and different people. Every situation and every person you meet is an opportunity for you to grow and to move closer to your goals so grab them with both hands! Do something new and different every day – challenge yourself. It could be something as simple as taking a different route to work or as challenging as taking those flying lesions you always promised you would take. Make a note of the new and exciting things you did each day and record them in the activity sheet below. Note anything that was pleasing or you particularly enjoyed. Maybe it was a compliment you received about a quality you didn't realise you had, or perhaps it was the birdsong you heard early in the morning as you drank your tea or coffee. And finally, be grateful for every moment and every opportunity that life gives you and you will soon find your heart overflowing with joy!

"We tend to forget that happiness doesn't come as a result of getting something we don't have, but rather of recognizing and appreciating what we do have."
– Frederick Keonig

Activity: My Challenge Worksheet

Key Goals	New and Exciting Things	Things that Pleased Me / I Enjoyed / Am Grateful For
Monday		
Tuesday		
Wednesday		
Thursday		
Friday		
Saturday		
Sunday		

Enhancing Your Motivation and Engagement

Finally, let's look at some of the factors that can keep you motivated and engaged. Motivation and engagement compels you to do whatever it takes to achieve your goal. It gives you the passion to begin exploring what it is you really want to do in life, and gives you the courage to follow your dreams. Motivation also permits us to pick ourselves up and dust ourselves off when we get knocked back – it is a critical driver for success. As one quote claims, "Motivation will almost always beat mere talent."

There are many different models related to motivation. Some examples include Maslow's hierarchy of needs, McGregor's Theory X and Theory Y and Hertzberg's Motivation–Hygiene Theory. All of these theories share the same basic principles about motivation: that it is complex and that "one size fits all" is far too simplistic. People have emotional, social and intellectual needs which are different for each individual. You are the best judge as to what drives and motivates you. Hopefully, the exercises in this workbook will have given you some insight into what these are. In addition to the key drivers and motivators which propel you forward, there are factors which can enhance and factors which can detract from your motivation. By managing these different factors you will further increase your chances of success in reaching your goals.

Andrew Martin's Motivation and Engagement Wheel comprehensively captures these factors. He proposes that there are a number of thoughts and behaviours which enhance motivation and engagement, called "Motivation and Engagement Boosters", and there are a number of thoughts and behaviours which reduce motivation and engagement, which he calls "Motivation and Engagement Mufflers and Guzzlers" (see the model on the following page). He argues that you can improve your motivation and engagement by increasing the motivation and engagement boosters and reducing your motivation and engagement mufflers and guzzlers. Dr. Martin has developed a questionnaire which measures these different factors and you can find out more about this and other workplace motivation and engagement tools by logging onto www.lifelongachievement.com. An outline of the Motivation and Engagement Wheel is shown below, along with some simple strategies to address each area within the Wheel.

The Motivation and Engagement Wheel

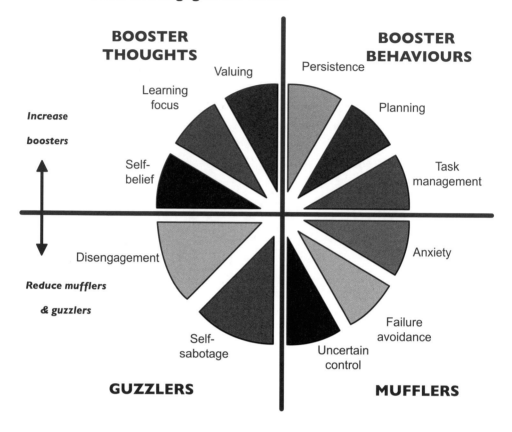

From the Motivation and Engagement Scale - Work (MES-W) and the Motivation and Engagement Workbook – Work (MEW-W). (www.lifelongachievement.com) by A. J. Martin, 2009, Sydney, Australia: Lifelong Achievement Group. Copyright 2009. Lifelong Achievement Group.

Motivation and Engagement Thoughts and Behaviours

M&E Areas	M&E Factors	Definition	Strategies to Address
Booster Thoughts	Self-belief	This relates to one's confidence and belief in their ability to do well and to perform to their best	Manage your negative self talk Recognise and celebrate your successes Provide opportunities for small wins
	Valuing	This relates to the belief that what you do has a value and is useful	Link what you learn at work to as many areas of your work (and beyond) as possible
	Learning Focus	This relates to being the best one can be. Individuals who are learning focused want to do a good job for its own sake and not just for rewards	Focus on doing your best and less on comparing yourself to others Aim for personal bests Look to continuously improve
Booster Behaviours	Planning	This relates to planning out your work task and keeping track of progress	Break down your work tasks into smaller segments Build contingencies into your work plans Frequently check the overall objectives with your current work output
	Task Management	This relates to every aspect of managing a task, including preparation, organising and timetabling work	Keep a record of what you do with your time in a week Identify where and when you work best and look to create more of these conditions
	Persistence	This relates to the doggedness with which one approaches a difficult or challenging activity	Identify blockers to the achievement of your goals and identify strategies to overcome them Be very clear on your goals and priorities

Motivation and Engagement Mufflers and Guzzlers

M&E Areas	M&E Factors	Definition	Strategies to Address
Mufflers	Anxiety	This relates to feeling nervous when they think about their work and worrying that they will perform poorly	Learn to recognise the signs of anxiety Adopt some relaxation techniques such as meditation, visualisation, deep breathing Develop practical strategies that will help you minimise anxiety e.g. preparing early
	Failure Avoidance	This relates to an individual mainly being motivated to avoid doing poorly or being seen to do poorly (rather than being motivated to do well).	Accept that mistakes are part of life's learning and can be the key to future success Focus on personal bests rather than failure avoidance
	Uncertain Control	This relates to an individual being unclear as to what should be done in order to perform well or what should be done to avoid failure	Focus on what you can control (e.g., your effort, your attitude) and develop these
Guzzlers	Self-Sabotage	This relates to doing things that reduce one's chances of success	Make a list of the types of things you do to self sabotage e.g. wasting time surfing the net, putting off doing a project, etc. Develop strategies to deal with these
	Disengagement	This relates to the feeling of giving up at work and feeling there is no point in trying at work	Develop a strong support network of people who can help and encourage you in your work Break your goals down into a series of smaller steps which are achievable when taken one part at a time

Your Motivation and Engagement Boosters, Mufflers and Guzzlers

List your Motivation and Engagement Boosters, Mufflers and Guzzlers in the box below. How do they support or detract from what you wish to achieve? What strategies or actions can you take to enhance your Booster Thoughts and Behaviours? What strategies or actions can you take to minimize and quell the Mufflers and Guzzlers? Who might be able to give you support?

My Motivations and Engagement Boosters, Mufflers and Guzzlers	Impact on My Actions, Thoughts or Behaviours	Actions I Could Take	People Who Could Help

Further Reading

BOOKS AND REFERENCE MATERIALS

Strategic Thinking and Planning

- *The Systems Thinking Approach to Strategic Planning and Management*, Stephen Haines (CRC Press LLC, 2000). Presents the first practical application of "systems thinking", a concept popularised by Peter Senge in *The Fifth Discipline*. Easy to follow approach to strategic thinking and integrated planning.

- *Strategic Thinking: A Step-By-Step Approach to Strategy*, Second Edition, Simon Wootton and Terry Horne (Kogan Page, 2004) Teaches the thinking skills required for sound strategic planning. Covers questions to ask and processes for formulating strategies and writing clear and concise strategic plans. Includes a CD-ROM with templates to facilitate strategic thinking and planning processes.

- "The Balanced Scorecard: Measures That Drive Performance", Kaplan and Norton (*Harvard Business Review*, January-February 1992). The Balanced Scorecard is a performance measurement system that can help managers to assess the performance of their organisation and predict future performance.

- *Exploring Corporate Strategy*, Johnson and Scholes (Prentice Hall, 2005). Contains detailed information on corporate and international strategy – this is a key text on corporate strategy and is illustrated with real life examples.

- *Delivering the Vision: Public Services for the Information Society and the Knowledge Economy*, Eileen Milner (Routledge, 2002). Explores the need for political vision, commitment and leadership if the shift from traditional forms of organisation to high-value, knowledge-intensive ones is to be safely negotiated.

- *Thinking Strategically: The Competitive Edge in Business, Politics and Everyday Life*, Avinash Dixit and Barry Nalebuff (W.W. Norton and Company, 1993). This book outlines the basics of good strategy making and how to apply strategic thinking in any area of your life. It was the *Financial Times* Top Ten book of the year in 1993, and equally relevant and entertaining today. Built on lots of case studies taken from business, sports, the movies, politics and gambling.

- *Built to Last: Successful Habits of Visionary Companies*, James Collins and Jerry Porras (Random House Business Books, 2005). In *Built to Last*, Collins and Porras study 18 visionary organisations that have survived in order to find out what sets successful organisations apart. This is an engaging read on the subject of strategy and strategic vision.

- *Focusing Partnerships: A Sourcebook for Municipal Capacity Building in Public-Private Partnership* (Municipal Capacity Building Series), Janelle Plummer, Chris Heymans (Earthscan Publications, 2002). Contributes to the PPP process debate by providing useful case studies and explaining how local government can establish effective relationships in public-private partnerships.

- *Strategic Thinking: A Four Piece Puzzle*, Bill Birnbaurm (Douglas Mountain Publishing, 2004). Strategy consultant Bill Birnbaum shares his lessons learned during 25 years helping management teams develop their business strategy. His anecdotal stories offer important lessons and the book is also an enjoyable read.

- *Harvard Business Review.* The world's acknowledged authority on business leadership and best management practices (online subscriptions at www.hbsp.harvard.edu).

- *Strategic Management Journal.* John Wiley and Sons (published 12 times a year. www.jstor.org),

- *Long Range Planning: The International Journal of Strategic Management.* www.lrp. ac. Provides useful information on the latest research and leading thinking in Strategic Management

Openness to Change

- *Managing the Unexpected: Assuring High Performance in an Age of Complexity,* Karl Weick and Kathleen Sutcliffe (John Wiley and Sons, 2001). A practical and solution-oriented approach to managing ambiguity and complexity. Includes numerous case studies demonstrating "mindful" practices and enables readers to assess and implement mindfulness in their own organisation.

- *Lessons from the Hive: The Buzz on Surviving and Thriving in an Ever-Changing Workplace*, Charles Decker (Dearborn Trade Publishing, 2004). A brief and powerful business fable about a fictional organisation that is learning positive ways of viewing ambiguity and organisational change. There are questions at the back of the book to assist reflection on each chapter.

- *Managing Transitions: Making the Most of Change* (2nd edition), William Bridges (William Bridges and Associates, 2003). "It isn't the changes that do you in, it's the transitions." Bridges describes the challenges of the three phases of transition and provides practical strategies for addressing the emotional needs of employees in each stage.

- *The Heart of Change: Real-Life Stories of How People Change Their Organizations*, John Kotter and Dan Cohen (Harvard Business School Press, 2002). Offers 34 instructive and vivid accounts of companies undergoing large-scale change. Chapters are organised by each of the eight stages of change identified by Kotter in his 1996 bestseller.

- *Leading in a Culture of Change*, Michael Fullan (Jossey-Bass, 2001). Debunks the notion of a "one-size-fits-all" blueprint for managing change. Provides insights into developing the core capabilities required for effective leadership under conditions of complex change.

- *Making Sense of Change Management: A Complete Guide to the Models, Tools & Techniques of Organizational Change*, Esther Cameron and Mike Green (Kogan Page, 2004). Explores the nature of change and the methods and techniques for managing it. Extensive information on organisational change, public relations techniques and crisis management.

- *Leading Change*, John Kotter (Harvard Business School Press, 1996). This important and enduring business manual provides a practical approach to an organised means of leading change. Presents a comprehensive eight-stage process of change that can be followed by managers at all levels.

- *Creating a Culture of Success: Fine-Tuning the Heart and Soul of Your Organization*, Charles Dygert and Richard Jacobs (Moo Press; 2nd edition, 2004). Serves as a road map through the minefields that keep an organisation going from where it is to where it wants to be. The authors propose the creation of a way of life, rather than simply a series of programmes.

- *Transforming Company Culture: Getting Your Company from Where You Are Now to Where You Want to Be*, David Drennan (McGraw-Hill, 1992). Remains one of the best texts available, combining insights about culture with practical tools, techniques and approaches for cascading strategic changes and creating buy-in at all levels of the organisation.

- *Balanced Scorecard Step-by-Step for Government and Nonprofit Agencies*, Paul Niven (John Wiley & Sons, 2003). Focusing directly on the public and not-for-profit sectors, this book helps these organisations overcome the unique challenges they face when implementing a Balanced Scorecard.

- *Breaking the Code of Change*, Michael Beer (Harvard Business School Press, 2000). Presents a series of articles incorporating two perspectives from which organisational change can be understood: one based on the creation of economic change, and one based on building long-term organisational capabilities.

- *International Journal of Business Performance Management.* Examines both hard and soft perspectives in managing business performance.

Creativity and Innovation

- *How To Have Creative Ideas: 62 Exercises to Develop the Mind,* Edward De Bono (Vermilion, 2007). This is a compact workbook which gives you great ideas to develop the skill of creative thinking. De Bono outlines 62 different games and exercises, using random words as a provocation to encourage creativity and lateral thinking.

- *The Mind Map Book: How to Use Radiant Thinking to Maximize your Brain's Untapped Potential,* Tony Buzan & Barry Buzan, (Plume, 1996). Tony & Barry Buzan here provide you with all the tools you need to release the full potential of your mind. It is packed with information and exercises that will radically change the way you think and use your mind.

- www.thespeedthinkingzone.com. The Speed Thinking Zone was founded by Dr. Ken Hudson. The purpose of this Zone is to help you to think in a better and faster way.

- *Anyone Can Do It: Building Coffee Republic from Our Kitchen Table,* Sahar Hashemi and Bobby Hashemi (Capstone, 2002). This is a useful guide for individuals who are looking to start up a new business and want useful ideas or insights as to how to go about it. It is structured around 57 "real life" laws derived from Sahar and Bobby Hashemis' experience in founding Coffee Republic.

- *The Necessary Revolution,* Peter Senge, Bryan Smith, Nina Kruschwitz, Joe Laur, Sara Schley. (Doubleday, 2008). This book focuses on the challenge for businesses to invest in new solutions to environmental problems and to apply innovative strategies that will generate both short- and long-term profitability while helping to create a better world.

- *Serious Creativity,* Edward de Bono (HarperCollins, 1992). Edward de Bono is a champion of creative techniques. This book is a rich guide to this process and how you can utilise your creativity to best effect.

- *Living the 7 Habits: The Courage to Change,* Stephen Covey (First Fireside, 1999). Covey presents 70 short stories of people as they meet challenges and practice the 7 Habits. The stories are organised into four areas labeled Individual, Family, Community & Education and Workplace. He pulls the different strands of the story together through commentary.

- *Nuts – Southwest Airline's Crazy Recipe for Business & Personal Success.* Kevin & Jackie Freiberg (Broadway Books, 2003). This book explains how Southwest Airlines can be so NUTS and so successful at the same time. This is a thinking and acting "out of the box" approach to organising and working that has demonstrated outstanding success and results. It is a highly enjoyable read packed with useful insights.

- *Leading the Revolution*, Gary Hamel (Harvard Business School Press, 2000). *Leading the Revolution* outlines an action plan for any company or individual wanting to become or remain innovative. It explains the underlying principles of innovation and details the necessary steps to becoming revolutionary.

- *The Creative Habit: Learn It and Use It for Life*, Twyla Tharp (Simon and Schuster Paperbacks, 2006). An entertaining "how to guide" that emphasises the work habits that leads to creative success.

- *Innovation and Entrepreneurship*, Peter Drucker (Harper & Row, 1985). Drucker, one of the most respected management thinkers of the twentieth century, puts together a practical book that explains what businesses, public service organisations and new ventures have to know, have to learn and have to do to be successful in today's economy and marketplace.

- *The Tipping Point*, Malcolm Gladwell (First Back Bay, 2002). The tipping point is that magic moment when an idea, trend or social behaviour crosses a threshold, tips and spreads like wildfire. Gladwell shows how the simplest of ideas can catch on and change the direction of life forever.

- *Make Us More Innovative: Critical Factors for Innovation Success*, Jeffrey Phillips (iUniverse books, 2008). Phillips provides a clear, sensible approach for transforming ideas into products, processes or new business strategies. If you've ever had the experience of seeing your ideas collapse before they've been given a chance to live, you need to read this book.

- www.brainstorming.co.uk. This website covers a host of ideas on brainstorming as well as a variety of other techniques for unlocking creativity, links to other sites, journals and publications.

- *Managing Creativity and Innovation* (Harvard Business Essentials, Harvard Business School Publishing Corporation, 2003). Covers the manager's role in sparking organisational creativity and provides useful insights into what managers and leaders must do in order to harness ambiguity and increase successful innovations.

Proficiency in Area of Expertise

- *Truth About Managing Your Career, And Nothing But the Truth*, Karen Otazo (Prentice Hall, 2006). This book is easy to read and provides 60 easy career management techniques that you can use. It gives hints and tips on working more smoothly with your manager, building networks, managing your workload, etc.

- *Lessons of Experience: How Successful Executives Develop on the Job*, Morgan McCall (Lexington, 1988). This book, based on information from 191 accomplished and high-potential executives, describes key developmental events and the lessons that can be learned from them. The lessons are grouped into themes and represent fundamental executive skills and ways of thinking. A sample of the themes and their related lessons include Setting and Implementing Agendas, Handling Relationships and Basic Values.

- "A Brand Called You", Tom Peters, *Fast Company Magazine*, August/September 1997. This article encapsulates the role of individuals in modern day teams and virtual teams. This much cited work encourages individuals to take as much care developing a brand for themselves as companies do, and to make themselves invaluable to their employers by becoming an expert in their field.

- *Job Shift: How to Prosper In a Workplace Without Jobs*, William Bridges (Perseus Books, 1994). This book was a seminal piece of writing regarding the world of work and careers. It clearly predicated the demise of the job and the traditional career back in the 1990s. The truths in this book are even more relevant in today's climate – a must read for those who wish to redefine their view of the world of work and of traditional careers.

- *Keeping Your Career on Track: Twenty Success Strategies*, Craig Chappelow & Jean Brittain Leslie (CCL Press, 2000). Managers who achieve significant professional goals do not often worry about career derailment. But complacency is not the same as continued success, which can usually be found among four leadership competencies: interpersonal relationships, team leadership, getting results and adaptability. Leadership success, achieving it and continuing it, depends heavily on developing and using each of these skills.

Problem Solving and Decision Making

- *Winning Decisions: Getting It Right the First Time*, J. Edward Russo & Paul J.H. Schoemaker (Piatkus Books, 2002). A book illustrating several decision-making strategies. It is easy to read, easy to follow and packed with applications, tools and solutions.

- "The Seasoned Executive's Decision Making Style", Kenneth R. Broussequ, Michael J. Driver, Gary Hourihan, Rikard Lasson (*Harvard Business Review*, February 2006). Research is showing that senior managers analyse and act on problems far differently than their more junior colleagues. This article outlines the approach that they take and how you can be left behind if your decision making does not advance.

- "The Hidden Traps in Decision Making," John S. Hammond, Ralph Keeney, Howard Raiffa (*Harvard Business Review*, January 2006). In making decisions you may be at the mercy of your mind's strange workings. This article shows how to catch thinking traps before they become judgement disasters.

- *Why Decisions Fail: Avoiding the Blunders and Traps That Lead to Debacles*, Paul C. Nutt (Berrett-Koehler Publishers, 2002). This book illustrates real-life case studies to tell the stories behind such famous debacles as the Millennium Dome, EuroDisney, Shell's disposal of the Brent Spar and Barings Bank.

- *The Decision-Making Pocket Book*, Neil Russell-Jones (Management Pocketbooks, 2000). This is a practical introduction to the techniques of decision-making which covers everything you need to know, from understanding the key components of a decision to a framework for decision-making with methodologies and case studies.

- *Judgement in Managerial Decision-Making*, M.H. Bazerman (John Wiley & Sons, 2002). This book shows readers how to identify their own biases in order to make better decisions, and teaches decision-making by involving the reader in decision quizzes.

- *Sixth Sense*, Kees van der Heijden (John Wiley & Sons, 2002). This book helps managers move beyond the idea that the future of business will resemble the past and allows them to use scenarios to imagine multiple perspectives. The concepts of organisational realities, experience and beliefs are explored to encourage and embrace change in business organisations for a successful future.

- *The Business Planning Pocketbook*, Neil Russell-Jones (Management Pocketbooks, 1998). A practical book that aims to boost business planning confidence. It explains what issues to address, how to write a business plan, what questions to ask, how much detail to include and the timeframe to adopt.

- "Stop Making Plans, Start Making Decisions", Michael C. Mankins & Richard Steele (*Harvard Business Review*, January, 2006). This article looks at how you can create a process that will really help you make informed decisions. It explores how the strategic planning process may be sidestepped because senior executives believe it is not focusing on what is important.

- Society for Judgment and Decision-Making. www.sjdm.org. The Society for Judgment and Decision-Making is an interdisciplinary academic organisation dedicated to the study of normative, descriptive and prescriptive theories of decision-making.

Action Oriented

- *Sixth Sense*, Kees van der Heijden (John Wiley & Sons, 2002). This book helps managers move beyond the idea that the future of business will resemble the past and allows them to use scenarios to imagine multiple perspectives. The concepts of organisational realities, experience, and beliefs are explored to encourage and embrace change in business organisations for a successful future.

- *Empowering People*, Jane Smith (Kogan Page, 1996). A highly practical guide to employee empowerment which contains a variety of tools, exercises and information on the topic.

- *The Empowered Manager: Positive Political Skills at Work*, Peter Block (Jossey-Bass, 1987). Peter Block provides a route to empowerment for managers via the use of positive political skills, beating the pressures of work that can erode creativity and initiative.

- *Hidden Value: How Great Companies Achieve Extraordinary Results with Ordinary People*, Charles O'Reilly III and Jeffrey Pfeffer (Harvard Business School Press, 2000). Pfeffer and O'Reilly III challenge the prevailing wisdom that companies must chase and acquire top talent to achieve success. Instead, they argue that organisations must exploit latent talent in their existing workforce.

- *Peak Performance: Aligning Hearts and Minds of Your Employees*, Jon R. Katzenbach (Harvard Business School Press, 2000). Jon Katzenbach, expert on teams and leadership, uses case studies to address the issue of achieving peak performance from individuals, and develops a theory which sets out five main paths towards building and sustaining exceptional levels of employee performance.

Goal Focused

- *The Human Side of Enterprise,* Douglas McGregor *(1960)*. McGregor's Theory X & Y are commonly used in the field of business and motivation. And though some of the ideas expressed in this theory are now considered a bit rigid, it still presents a very strong foundation from which to understand human motivation.

- *The Art of Exceptional Living,* Jim Rohn (Nightingale Conant, 2003). Jim Rohn is one of the most respected speakers on the management circuit. He has influenced literally thousands of people to take control and realise success in their lives. In this inspirational book, Rohn shows us how to truly live our lives in a way that brings true success and happiness.

- *The Personal Efficiency Program: How to Get Organised to Do More Work in Less Time*, K. Gleeson (John Wiley & Sons 2000). Great book for focusing your mind on what needs to be done and helping you plan what is important.

- *How to Get Control of Your Time and Life*, A. Lakein (Gower Page, 1987). A practical guide to taking control of your life and your time with some useful hints and tips as well as some exercises.

- *Get Everything Done and Still Have Time to Play*, Mark Foster (Help Yourself, 2000). This book contains a variety of examples and tools to help readers find an effective system for organising themselves and managing their time.

- *Time Management 24/7: How to Double Your Effectiveness*, Simon Phillips (McGraw-Hill Business, 2002). This book approaches the issue of time management from a 21st century perspective. It also contains a host of tools and models that take you, step-by-step, through Phillips' 24/7 system.

- *The Business Planning Pocketbook*, Neil Russell-Jones (Management Pocketbooks, 1998). A practical book that aims to boost business planning confidence. It explains what issues to address, how to write a business plan, what questions to ask, how much detail to include and the timeframe to adopt.

- www.goal-setting-guide.com. This site offers tools and resources on goal setting and motivation to help you achieve your true potential.

- www.Effectivemeetings.com. This is a very good website on handling effective meetings.

Authentic Leadership

- *The Servant as Leader*, Robert K. Greenleaf (Robert K Greenleaf Centre, 1991). An inspiring book on leadership that challenges one's thinking on the topic. It outlines the ten characteristics necessary for leadership.

- *One Minute Manager*, Kenneth Blanchard and Spencer Johnson (Blanchard Family Partnership, 1982). This book is a classic on how you can manage effectively the many demands that you have on your time. It is simple and easy to read and gets its message across as a story.

- *The Empowered Manager: Positive Political Skills at Work*, Peter Block (Jossey Bass, 1987). Looking at a wide variety of organisations, Block outlines how managers and organisations can renewed and reenergise themselves by allowing their people to flourish and release their vision and manage the demands that are placed on them.

- "Anatomy of a Leader: Where are the Leaders of Tomorrow?" Genevieve Capowski, *Management Review*, 1994, pp. 10–17. This short article clearly outlines how leadership cannot be taught but can be released in all of us if we would only take the time to find our true voice.

- *Leadership Blind Spots and What to Do About Them*, Karen Blakely (John Wiley & Sons, 2007). This is an excellent book on Leadership Development. It clearly explains how leaders can challenge themselves to perform at their peak. There are many practical examples of how to maximise learning agility to reach one's true potential. Any leader who implements the practices outlined in this book will immediately improve their ability to perform in today's highly competitive global environment.

- *On Character and Servant-Leadership: Ten Characteristics of Effective, Caring Leaders*, Larry Spears (Clearinghouse for Leadership Programs, 2000). This book takes Greenberg's ideas and concepts on leadership and brings them to life. It gives many wonderful examples of the ten characteristics in practice.

- *Good to Great*, Jim Collins (Harper Business, 2001). Following five years of research Jim Collins argues in *Good to Great* that the success of any organisation is more closely linked to the qualities of the leader than initially thought. A "Level 5" leader is what takes companies from being good to great.

- *Peak Performance: Aligning Hearts and Minds of Your Employees*, Jon R. Katzenbach (Harvard Business School Press, 2000). Jon Katzenbach, expert on teams and leadership, uses case studies to address the issue of achieving peak performance from individuals, and develops a theory which sets out five main paths towards building and sustaining exceptional levels of employee performance.

- *Primal Leadership: Realizing the Power of Emotional Intelligence*, Daniel Goleman, Annie McKee and Richard E. Boyatzis (Harvard Business School Press, 2002). Best-selling emotional intelligence researcher Daniel Goleman and his fellow authors further investigate emotional intelligence, this time focusing on emotionally intelligent leadership.

- *Discovering the Leader in You: A Guide to Realizing Your Personal Leadership Potential*, Robert Lee and Sara King (Jossey-Bass Publishers, 2001). Many executives find themselves in leadership roles by default and then discover they are just not personally suited to them. Through examples, exercises and research results, this book offers an intentional way for leaders, and those who aspire to be, to match leadership roles with their personal preferences and capabilities.

- *Why Managers Have Trouble Empowering*, Wilfred Drath (CCL Press, 1993). Why do many successful managers have trouble empowering their subordinates even though they are sincerely committed to doing so? This report suggests that the strengths that have made the manager successful – for instance, the ability to act decisively – may have concomitant weaknesses – for instance, a tendency not to value the opinions of others – that limit their ability to be empowering. To address this, managers must examine their own personal development at the level of personal meaning, and organisations must evolve into institutions that support such development.

- *Shackleton's Way: Leadership Lessons from the Great Antarctic Explorer*, Margot Morrell and Stephanie Capparell, with a preface by Alexandra Shackleton (Nicholas Brealey, 2001). This book uses the great explorer Sir Ernest Shackleton as a leadership model. It is an eminently practical guide to leadership combined with a fascinating historical narrative.

- *Coaching for Leadership: The Practice of Leadership Coaching from the World's Greatest Coaches*, Marshall Goldsmith and Laurence Lyons (Pfeiffer, 2005). This book reflects recent changes in coaching practices, includes well-researched best practices and provides additional guidance and tools from the greatest leadership coaches from around the world. Each chapter addresses a proven application, offers key principles of practice and highlights critical learning points.

- *On Becoming a Leader*, Warren Bennis (Arrow, 1998). Bennis is a prolific thinker and writer on leadership. This book explains how people become leaders and how they lead. It also looks at how organisations can encourage or stifle potential leaders. It is based on interviews with leaders from a wide range of fields, including business, law, medicine and the film industry.

- *The 3 Keys to Empowerment: Release the Power Within People for Astonishing Results*, Ken Blanchard, John Carlos and Alan Randolph (McGraw-Hill, 1999). A guide for managers, giving detailed answers to frequently asked questions concerning the route to empowerment.

- *Harvard Business Review on Managing People* (Harvard Business School Press, 2000). This book contains a number of leading articles from the *Harvard Business Review* concerning people management. Included is an article by Chris Argyris, "Empowerment: The Emperor's New Clothes".

- www.greenleaf.org. Comprehensive information on servant leadership and other related topics including seminars, training and retreats.

- www.pfdf.org. This site has a huge array of information and insights into leadership and management.

Communication and Influence

- *Getting to Yes: Negotiating Agreement Without Giving In*, Roger Fisher, William Ury and Bruce Patton (Penguin Books, 2005). Since original publication in 1981, *Getting to Yes* has sold over one million copies in its various editions. A universal guide to the art of negotiating personal and professional disputes. It offers a concise strategy for coming to mutually acceptable agreements in every sort of conflict.

- *Heart of a Leader: Insights on the Art of Influence*, Ken Blanchard (Cook Communications, 2005). Ken Blanchard, of *The One Minute Manager* fame, helps readers discover the art of influence through the greatest life and leadership lessons he learned as an educator and business leader.

Further Reading

- *Working with Emotional Intelligence*, Daniel Goleman (Bantam, 2000). Transfers into the workplace the concepts from his bestseller, *Emotional Intelligence*. Explains why emotional intelligence counts more than IQ or expertise for excelling on the job, and describes 12 personal competencies and 13 key relationship skills.

- *Corporate Conversations: A Guide to Crafting Effective and Appropriate Internal Communications*, Shel Holtz (Amacom, 2003). Shows how to take a strategic approach to managing and implementing organisational communications. Covers various types of communication and provides tools for organising, budgeting and measuring the value of communication.

- *Great Communication Secrets of Great Leaders*, John Baldoni (McGraw-Hill, 2003). Selects some of the most persuasive people from the twentieth century and analyses their secrets. Also develops guidelines for making the most of computer-aided presentations and other new technologies.

- *20 Communication Tips at Work: A Quick and Easy Guide to Successful Business Relationships*, Eric Maisel (New World Library, 2001). The 20 tips include advice on how to offer critical feedback, understand messages, sort out motivations, offer praise and keep people informed. Brief exercises help readers assess their own communication skills.

- *Business Communication* (Harvard Business Essentials) (Harvard Business School Press, 2003). How to communicate effectively for every business situation, from sensitive feedback to employees to persuasive communications for customers. Offers advice for improving writing skills, oral presentations and one-on-one dealings with others.

- *E-Writing: 21st Century Tools for Effective Communication*, Dianna Booher (Pocket Books). Describes how to become an eloquent writer for the digital age. Covers combating counterproductive e-mail habits, writing authoritatively and persuasively, and selecting an appropriate style for the audience you're addressing.

- *Introducing NLP*, Joseph O'Connor and John Semour (Mandala, 1990). This book gives you practical skills in how to be an excellent communicator. It is a nice introduction to NLP and easy to read and understand.

- *Making Presentations* (DK Essential Managers), Tim Hindle (DK Adult, 1999). Thumbnail guide to all aspect of making presentations. Also contains tips, sample material and checklists which make the whole process quick and easy to follow.

Building Relationships

- *The 29% Solution*, Ivan R. Misner and Michelle R. Donovan (Greenleaf Book Press, 2008). This book will help you develop your networking skills, increase your connections and become part of the roughly 29 per cent of people who are, in fact, separated from the rest of the world by just six degrees.

- *Breakthrough Networking: Building Relationships That Last*, Second Edition, Lillian Bjorseth (Duoforce Enterprises, 2003). An excellent text for all professionals who seriously wish to improve their interpersonal and networking skills. Includes sections on understanding your networking style, managing impressions and interpreting body language.

- *The Relationship Edge in Business: Connecting with Customers and Colleagues When It Counts*, Jerry Acuff (John Wiley & Sons, 2004). Outlines a simple three step process and how to use it to influence, persuade and build meaningful relationships with people who are crucial to our success.

- *The Ripple Effect: Maximizing the Power of Relationships for Life & Business*, Steve Harper (SWOT Publishing, 2005). Affirms the way people should behave in the business world and speaks to treating employees, customers and associates as people first and foremost, rather than as tools to an end.

- *Winning with People: Discover the People Principles that Work for You Every Time*, John Maxwell (Nelson Business, 2005). The book offers 25 chapter-based "People Principles" that explore how to approach interpersonal and business relationships, and create win-win relationships and partnerships.

- *What Got You Here Won't Get You There*, Marshall Goldsmith with Mark Reiter (Hyperion, 2008). The corporate world is full of intelligent and skilled executives, but few will ever reach the top and, according to Goldsmith, subtle nuances make the difference.

- *The Speed of Trust*, Stephen M.K. Covey (Pocket Books, 2008). This book argues that "prioritizing trust – actively seek to establish it, grow it, restore it, and wisely extend it – will bring personal and organisational dividends that far exceed any other path." Although it has value for everyone, this book is especially helpful and important reading for those in leadership positions.

- *First Impressions: What You Don't Know About How Others See You*, Ann Demarius and Valerie White (Bantam Dell, 2004). Writing in accessible self-help style, the authors identify the "seven fundamentals of first impressions". These seven chapters make up the meat of the book. The authors discuss different ways in which you can enhance the impression you make.

Co-operative Teamwork

- *Resolving Conflicts at Work: Eight Strategies for Everyone on the Job,* Kenneth Cloke, Joan Goldsmith, Warren Bennis (Jossey-Bass, 2005). Outlines eight strategies that show how the inevitable disputes and divisions in the workplace actually provide an opportunity for greater creativity, productivity, enhanced morale and personal growth.

- *Great Business Teams*, Howard M. Guttman (John Wiley & Sons, 2008). Howard M. Guttman takes you inside some of the word's most successful corporations to discover how a powerful new high-performance horizontal model has changed the way leaders lead, team members function, challenges are met and decisions are made.

- *The Five Dysfunctions of a Team*, Patrick M. Lencioni (Jossey Bass, 2002). *The Five Dysfunctions of a Team* is written as a "leadership fable", a story of a technology company that is struggling in the marketplace to find customers. Although written as a fable, the book provides practical advice, which leaders can use in their own teams. The book is easy to read and the model provided is simple to understand making it a powerful tool for helping teams improve.

- *Team Roles at Work*, Meredith Belbin (Butterworth Heinemann, 1993). *Team Roles at Work* provides an ideal practical guide to Belbin Team Roles. Find out how to apply the nine Belbin Team Roles in a practical setting. Operational strategies provide ideas, techniques and a new range of information and advice which can be used to the advantage of the organisation.

- *The Wisdom of Teams*, Katzenbach and Smith (HarperBusiness, 1994). An excellent book, highly recommended for all project professionals, since it takes a different tack than the average book on teambuilding. It is especially important for project managers interested in the area of leadership. It is a very useful compilation of information about what makes an effective team.

- *Quick Team Building Activities for Busy Managers: 50 Exercises That Get Results in Just 15 Minutes*, Brian Cole Miller (Amacom, 2004). This guide offers 50 proven exercises any manager can use without spending lots of money. These group activities are designed with the non-trainer in mind. It features a special chapter on troubleshooting and dealing with unexpected difficulties in team building.

- *The Performance Factor – Unlocking the Secrets of Team Work*, Pat MacMillan (B&H Publishing Group, 2001). Team resource expert Pat MacMillan discusses the characteristics of a high performance team and how to implement a new paradigm of leadership to bring any organisation to greater efficiency.

- *Team Work is an Individual Skill: Getting Your Work Done When Sharing Responsibility*, Christopher Avery, Meri Aaron Walker and Erin O'Toole Murphy (Berrett-

Koehler Publishers, 2001). This book aims to remove the ambiguity that exists around team building by focusing on five core abilities. It also shows that teamwork is an individual responsibility and skill set, not a group process, and shows how a person can be powerful when sharing responsibility to get things done.

- *Leading High Impact Teams: The Coach Approach to Peak Performance.* Cynder Niemela and Rachael Lewis (High Impact Publishing, 2001). It inspires team leaders to use the "Coach Approach" to make their team experiences lighter, more synergistic and infinitely more productive. Full of practical, step-by-step activities, real life stories and anecdotes, you'll learn what it takes to lead or coach a team to high impact.

- www.fastcompany.com. Fast Company provides excellent site search facilities for searching for teams-related articles.

Positive Attitude

- *Resilience: The Power to Bounce Back When the Going Gets Tough*, F. Flach (Hartherleigh, 1997). This book highlights how we can get stuck in our own negativity rather than turning situations around to our advantage.

- *The 4-Hour Workweek: Escape 9-5, Live Anywhere, and Join the New Rich*, Timothy Ferriss (Crown, 2007). The four-hour workweek is a semi-autobiographical self-help book on how to automate your life and your business and free up your time to do what it is your really want to do.

- *Learned Optimism: How to Change Your Mind and Your Life*, Martin E. P. Seligman (Vintage Books, 2006). This gives you the complete ABCDE method for developing optimism in your life.

- *Outliers: The Story of Success*, Malcolm Gladwell (Little Brown, 2008). Gladwell takes a close look at what makes for high levels of success and presents some interesting findings for the reader to ponder.

- *Adjusting the Sails: Resilience Strategies for Professionals*, M.L. Lightner (M & M Discoveries, 2000). Some great insights into how you can put action plans in place to help you develop more resilience. Has some useful resilient strategies that you can employ.

- *Wellness at Work: Building Resilience to Job Stress*, V. O'Hara (New Harbinger Publishers, 1995). Comprehensive review about wellness and work, what it means and how you can build it into your every day life and the life of your organisation.

- *Building Resiliency: How to Thrive in Times of Change*, Mary Lynn Pulley and Michael Wakefield (CCL Press, 2001). This guidebook defines resiliency, explains why it's important, and describes how you can develop your own store of resiliency.

It focuses on nine developmental components that, taken together, create a sense of resiliency and increase your ability to handle the unknown and to view change – whether from disappointment or success – as an opportunity for development.

- *The Complete Guide to Stress Management*, Chandra Patel (Vermilion, 1996). This remains perhaps the most successful book available on stress management. It looks at the causes and symptoms of stress and suggests a series of exercises and relaxation techniques which help to alleviate the harmful effects of stress.

- *Managing Workplace Stress*, Steve Williams and Lesley Cooper (John Wiley & Sons, 2002). This is a highly informative book that is both easy to read and understand. It educates you about the causes and results of stress and provides workable solutions for combating stress in the workplace.

- *The Big Book of Stress Relief Management Games: Quick, Fun Activities for Feeling Better at Work*, Robert Epstein (McGraw-Hill Education, 2000). There are 50 stress relief and relaxation games and exercises within this book. The games and exercises can be used effectively to lighten up meetings, boost morale and help everyone unwind after a hard week.

- *The Power of Positive Thinking*, Norman Vincent Peele (Fireside, 1980). This is an oldie but a goodie on staying and remaining positive. It has lots of useful insights and ideas as to how you can transform your thinking.

- *The Seven Habits of Highly Effective People*, Stephen Covey (Free Press, 1989). In this hugely popular book Stephen Covey outlines the seven key habits of highly effective people. This is an easy to read book and will provide you with the keys to being successful. There is also a workbook to accompany this book which makes developing the habits simple and easy.

- *The Eight Habits*, Stephen Covey (Free Press, 2004). Finding our voice and helping others to find theirs is what the 8th Habit is all about. The 8th Habit is about the soul's yearning for greatness, the organisation's search for significance and results, and humanity's search for its voice. The 8th Habit shows the way to greatness.

- www.somats.com/epa1997.htm. Online article which discusses the link between emotional intelligence and physical well-being.

Self and Other Awareness

- *Emotional Intelligence*, Daniel Goleman (Bloomsbury, 1995). The book that brought the term emotional intelligence to the public consciousness. Goleman synthesises the work of influential writers such as Gardner, Mayer and Salovey into a digestible explanation of EQ.

- *Working with Emotional Intelligence*, Daniel Goleman (Bantam Doubleday, 2000). In the follow-up to *Emotional Intelligence*, Goleman suggests a performance-based model for EQ. He demonstrates how the principles of EQ can be applied to improve organisational performance.

- *NLP Workbook: A Practical Guide to Achieving What You Want*, Joseph O'Connor (Thorsons, 2001). This workbook is a basic, at-home NLP course, providing easy-to-follow exercises and reflections to which the reader can return time and again. It addresses topics such as How to Change Emotional State, The Power of Language and Getting Results, and can be applied to all kinds of different areas, e.g. business, sport, health. *The NLP Workbook* is designed to be a basic manual for the beginner in NLP, and also a clear and easy reference manual for practitioners and trainers.

- *Introducing NLP* (Neuro Linguistic Programming), Joseph O'Connor and John Seymore (Mandala, 1990). This handbook describes in simple terms what gifted people do differently, and enables the reader to learn these patterns of excellence. This approach gives the practical skills used by outstanding communicators.

- *Primal Leadership: Realizing the Power of Emotional Intelligence*, Daniel Goleman, Annie McKee and Richard E. Boyatzis (Harvard Business School Press, 2002). Best-selling emotional intelligence researcher Daniel Goleman and his fellow authors further investigate emotional intelligence, this time focusing on emotionally intelligent leadership.

- *Raising Your Emotional Intelligence: A Practical Guide*, Jeanne Segal (Henry Holt, 1997). Dr. Jeanne Segal's book offers advice and techniques to raise EQ. It is simple and easy to use and contains many great insights and offerings on the topic.

- *Executive EQ: Emotional Intelligence in Leadership and Organisation*, Robert Cooper and Ayman Sawaf (Perigee, 1998). This book explores the role of EQ in effective leadership, offering advice for personal development.

- *Emotional Intelligence at Work*, Hendrie Weisinger (Jossey-Bass, 2000). Weisinger outlines the core competencies of emotional intelligence, demonstrating how they can be developed to improve personal effectiveness.

- www.eqi.org. Comprehensive site featuring articles and resources on emotional intelligence.

- www.opp.eu.com. Covers a comprehensive range of personality and other assessment material.

- www.somats.com/epa1997.htm. Online article which discusses the link between emotional intelligence and physical well-being.

- www.brainbench.com. This site requires you to register, but once registered, it is possible to take their free online personality test.

Personal Commitment

- *The Seven Habits of Highly Effective People*, Stephen Covey (Free Press, 1989). In this hugely popular book Stephen Covey outlines the seven key habits of highly effective people. This is an easy to read book and will provide you with the keys to being successful. There is also a workbook to accompany this book which makes developing the habits simple and easy.

- *In Search of Excellence: Lessons from America's Best-Run Companies*, Thomas Peters and Robert Waterman (First Harper Business Essentials, 2004). This phenomenal bestseller is based on a study of 43 of America's best-run companies from a diverse array of business sectors. Describes eight basic principles of management that made these organisations successful.

- *The 8th Habit: From Effectiveness to Greatness*, Stephen Covey, (Free Press, 2004). Finding our voice and helping others to find theirs is what the 8th Habit is all about. The 8th Habit is about the soul's yearning for greatness, the organisation's search for significance and results, and humanity's search for its voice. The 8th Habit shows the way to greatness.

- *Smart Management: Using Politics in Organisations*, David Butcher and Martin Clarke (Palgrave Macmillan, 2001). Describes the generally negative view of organisational politics as a misunderstanding. Demonstrates how understanding and managing organisational politics can have extremely powerful positive effects.

- *Time Management 24/7: How to Double Your Effectiveness*, Simon Phillips (McGraw-Hill Business, 2002). This book approaches the issue of time management very much from a 21st century perspective. It also contains a host of tools and models that take you, step-by-step, through Phillips' 24/7 system.

- *Get Everything Done and Still Have Time to Play*, Mark Foster (Help Yourself, 2000). A fantastic book on time management. It contains a variety of examples and tools to help readers find an effective system for organising themselves and managing their time.

- *The Motivation Handbook*, Sarah Hollyforde and Steve Whiddett (CIPD, 2002). This book will help you gain a clear understanding of how and why people can be turned on (and off) and how to create the conditions to optimise performance. The authors look at motivation theory, such as Maslow and Herzberg, and how you can apply this in your organisation to create the conditions that will ensure that you want to deliver winning performance.

- www.goal-setting-guide.com. This site offers tools and resources on goal setting and motivation to help you achieve your true potential.

Self-confidence and Self-belief

- *Assertiveness at Work: A Practical Guide to Handling Awkward Situations*, Ken Back and Kate Back (McGraw-Hill, 1999). Designed specifically for managers, this book offers practical guidance on how you can handle difficult situations at work through demonstrating assertiveness.

- *Super Confidence*, Gael Lindenfield (Thorsons, 1989). This book gives practical hints and tips on how to communicate effectively in order to create a positive self-image and improve your confidence.

- *Perfect Assertiveness*, Jan Ferguson (Random House Business Books, 2003). This book gives a comprehensive introduction to the psychological issues of assertiveness and aggression. There is also practical guidance on how to better understand your own behaviour and increase your assertiveness.

- *Develop Your Assertiveness* (2nd edition), Sue Bishop (Kogan Page, 2000). This book is presented in a "workshop style" with lots of advice, case studies and exercises to help you become more assertive. It will help you improve your effectiveness in particular circumstances,

Openness to Learning

- *The Learning Styles Questionnaire 2006 – 80 Item Version,* Peter Honey & Alan Mumford (Peter Honey Publications, 2006). This book provides individuals with all the tools they need to identify their preferred learning style(s), to select learning opportunities that suit stronger style(s) and to develop weaker styles. It also contains information on the Learning Cycle, as well as the 80-item Learning Styles Questionnaire and scoring.

- *Experiential Learning: Experience as the Source of Learning and Development*, David Kolb (Prentice Hall, 1984). Here David Kolb develops his theory of learning styles, and experiential learning, dealing with the learning cycle and experiential learning techniques. This is the classic text on the topic.

- *Hidden Value: How Great Companies Achieve Extraordinary Results with Ordinary People*, Charles O'Reilly III and Jeffrey Pfeffer (Harvard Business School Press, 2000). Pfeffer and O'Reilly III challenge the prevailing wisdom that companies must chase and acquire top talent to achieve success. Instead, they argue that organisations must exploit latent talent in their existing workforce.

- *Coaching for Performance*, John Whitmore (Nicholas Brearley Books, 1996). This coaching guide is the home of the GROW model outlined in the Models and

Strategies Element of this unit. Whitmore explores a philosophy of coaching without insisting on its use. This is the latest edition, including examples of question use for generating awareness and responsibility, and new sections on learning, enjoyment and motivation.

- *Co-Active Coaching: New Skills for Coaching People Toward Success in Work and Life*, Laura Whitworth (Henry House et al, Davies-Black Publishing, 1998). Laura Whitworth and Henry House are the co-founders of the Coaches Training Institute, one of the main coaching qualification centres in the US. In this book, they propose a coaching model, focusing on the coaching relationship, in which both coach and client are active collaborators.

- *Effective Coaching*, Myles Downey (Orion Business Books, 1999). A comprehensive introduction to effective coaching, including coaching skills, models and techniques. Myles Downey is a coach of 15 years' experience. In partnership with the Work Foundation, he set up the School of Coaching, which aims to develop the coaching capability of senior managers and executives. See above for a link to the site.

- *In Transition: From the Harvard Business School Club of New York's Career Management Seminar*, Mary Lindley Burton and Richard A Wedemeyer (Harper Business, 1992). Burton and Wedemeyer have conducted this seminar, open only to Harvard MBAs, for over 10 years and this book now makes the information available to everyone. It provides the basics of a self-marketing model for ambitious managers working their way up the corporate ladder.

- *Internalizing Strengths: An Overlooked Way of Overcoming Weaknesses in Managers*, Robert Kaplan (CCL Press, 1999). In this report, the author explains why it is critical to recognize strengths in order to improve performance and why it is often difficult to get that notion across to executives. For practicing managers and those who develop them, this report offers sound but often neglected developmental advice.

- *New Directions in Career Planning and the Workplace: Practical Strategies for Career Management Professionals*, Jean Kummerow (ed.) (Davies-Black Publishing, 2000). This book deals with career management from the point of view of an organisation. It delivers a collection of the most current thinking and practice on new approaches to career and life planning, work–life balance values clarification, multicultural career counselling, the impact of technology, and new applications of instruments such as Myers-Briggs Type Indicators and the Strong Interest Inventory. This edition also provides information about the way in which the workforce will develop over the next 10 years, and contains an examination of six businesses driving change in the workplace. *Developmental Assignments: Creat-*

ing Learning Experiences without Changing Jobs, Cynthia McCauley (CCL Press, 2006). This fieldbook is modelled after Eighty-Eight Assignments for Development in Place, one of CCL's most popular publications. The tables inside this book are full of assignments. You'll also find cross-references to CCL's assessment tools: 360 by Design, Executive Dimensions, Benchmarks, Prospector, and Skillscope. If you want to target the development of specific competencies as a result of receiving feedback from any of these, the cross-references will direct you to appropriate assignments.

- *Setting Your Development Goals: Start with Your Values*, Bill Sternbergh and Sloan Weitzel (CCL Press, 2001). This guidebook is about changing the way you think about setting goals. It is about identifying goals that are important and meaningful to five key areas of your life: career, self, family, community, and spirit. The goals you create will be SMART: specific, measurable, attainable, realistic, and timed. Setting meaningful goals will reward you with real progress toward success in all areas of your life.

- Learning Styles Questionnaire. www.peterhoney.com. This is the home of the famous Honey and Mumford Learning Styles Questionnaire. The site contains development tools that focus on learning and behaviour.

- Clutterbuck Associates. www.clutterbuckassociates.com. David Clutterbuck is an international authority on mentoring and learning at work, and is author of some 40 books on the subject. He offers useful hints and tips on Mentoring and Coaching.

- The School of Coaching. www.theworkfoundation.com/solutions/soc/new_home2.htm. The School of Coaching aims to develop the coaching capability of senior managers and executives.

- www.career-planning.com. This useful site offers career planning tests to assess participants' abilities and match them to their ideal career.

- Free Management Library. www.mapnp.org/library. The Management Assistance Program (MAP) hosts this free site. It provides a large amount of information on many management topics.

- Harvard Business School Publishing. www.hbsp.harvard.edu. Although the official site of Harvard Business School Publishing charges for most of its articles, it remains one of the best sources of cutting-edge performance management thinking on the web.